Praise for *You Are Worthy*

"From the moment you begin reading *You Are Worthy*, you will feel as if Kelley Holland is speaking to you, woman to woman. You will also find relatable stories from women on their own financial journeys, and step-by-step strategies to 'lift you as you climb.' Wherever you are in life, you will find helpful tools and strategies to design your future."

— HEATHER ETTINGER, founder and CEO of Luma Wealth and author of *Lumination: Shining a Light on a Woman's Journey to Financial Wellness*

"Kelley Holland's *You Are Worthy* invites women to take charge of their money and shows them how to envision, plan, and pursue their financial future. In this engaging and empowering how-to guide, Kelley breaks down concepts in everyday language and shares necessary action steps with real-life stories, examples, and reflections along the way. This book is an excellent resource for women who are just getting started and those who are seeking to enhance their financial planning."

— CATHERINE COLLINSON, CEO and president of Transamerica Institute and Transamerica Center for Retirement Studies

"*You Are Worthy* accomplishes something rare and powerful in giving equal importance to emotional awareness and financial knowledge in our dealings with money matters. It's a guide full of information and support that not only leads us to create our own unique financial plan but also brings healing to our money lives."

— KATE LEVINSON, PhD, author of *Emotional Currency: A Woman's Guide to Building a Healthy Relationship with Money*

"This book is what women need—a normalizing, practical, empowering, and hope-inspiring book about money. Kelley Holland warns women of the cost of keeping quiet about finances and gets the conversation started with extremely relatable financial stories from her clients. Her journaling exercises help us start reflecting on our own relationships with money. This book promotes financial consciousness of our past, present, and future, and is helpful for women at any stage of life."

—JOYCE MARTER, LCPC, author of *The Financial Mindset Fix: A Mental Fitness Program for an Abundant Life*

"This is a book every woman needs: an encouraging, empathetic guide to taking charge of our finances, one step at a time. Kelley Holland has deep insight into our emotional relationship to money and the financial challenges so many women face daily. With *You Are Worthy*, she has written a book that empowers, educates, and motivates readers to take action, no matter their age."

—SUSAN PEPIN, MD, MPH, Clinical Professor, College of Health Solutions, Arizona State University and Chair, YaleWomen

"Every woman who desires to be financially secure needs to read this book! In *You Are Worthy*, Holland expertly and compassionately reveals why women struggle with money. By teaching the simple fundamentals of making money work for you, she provides judgment-free advice and a practical roadmap on how to embrace a new future—regardless of your age or stage."

—DEBRA BOULANGER, CEO of The Great Do-Over

You Are Worthy

Change Your Money Mindset, Build Your Wealth, & Fund Your Future

Kelley Holland

SHE WRITES PRESS

Published 2022
Printed in the United States of America
Print ISBN: 978-1-64742-239-4
E-ISBN: 978-1-64742-240-0
Library of Congress Control Number: 2022905787

For information, address:
She Writes Press
1569 Solano Ave #546
Berkeley, CA 94707

Interior design by Tabitha Lahr

She Writes Press is a division of SparkPoint Studio, LLC.

For Henry, Anna, and Eleanor

May you find the world to be a wonderful place and
leave it even better for those who follow.

Contents

Introduction

Do you remember the last time you had a real conversation with a female friend about money?

I don't mean a casual exchange about what you spent on something. I mean an honest, in-depth conversation about your savings goals, your salary, your worries about your financial future, your day-to-day money challenges—your actual money life.

If you are like most women, your answer is never. Ever. And this book is for you.

The truth is that most women don't like to talk about money. Some 61 percent of women said in a 2018 survey that they would rather talk about death than money. When asked, these women may say it is impolite to talk about finances, or they don't feel knowledgeable. But for many, the underlying truth is that they just feel bad about their money lives.

Even women who are competent and successful in almost everything else they do often feel ashamed of their money habits, unsure where to turn for help, worried about their future financial security, or afraid to learn the true state of their finances.

THE COST OF KEEPING QUIET

Unfortunately, when we keep silent about our financial lives, we wind up carrying our money stress inside. We feel alone with our negative emotions. Our silence causes us pain—emotionally and physically.

It has other costs as well.

When we keep our money lives to ourselves, we never get to find out that many women around us are dealing with the same kinds of challenges. We never learn that some of our closest friends are also lying awake at night worried about their financial future. Often, we don't learn that our parents are struggling financially until the situation becomes a crisis.

We don't learn good news either. We don't find out that someone we know has figured out a great way to stay on a budget. We lose an opportunity to learn about investing together. We fail to learn what we deserve to be paid and how to ask for it. The world of investing remains cloaked in jargon we never learn to decipher.

When we are quiet, it also becomes easier for women's structural financial challenges to persist, from the gender pay gap to the glass ceiling and the implicit pressure on women to put their careers second and step back to care for children and elderly parents.

This is not to say that we are all a bunch of hapless damsels in distress. Far from it. More and more women are breadwinners, and some women do enter money conversations with confidence and happily take charge of their finances. But there are still many of us—including some breadwinners—who feel discomfort when it comes to our money and hold that feeling inside.

To be clear, women are *not* to blame for our silence—and certainly not for the persistence of the structural challenges we face, like the fact that we have to work fifteen-plus months to earn what men earn in a year. We start receiving implicit social messages that women are "bad with money" and "bad with numbers" at an early age. Our parents tend to talk to our brothers about money more than they talk to us. Only a minority of states require financial education in their schools, so for millions of girls there is no obvious time when actual education could counteract these forces. What on earth would make women want to expose our resulting feelings and beliefs in conversation?!

TIME FOR A NEW APPROACH

My goal with this book is to change all that.

I promise that by the time you reach the last page, you will feel less alone with your money challenges. You will understand why managing your money can feel so difficult and overwhelming. You will be inspired to take charge of your finances, and you'll have practical, achievable steps you can take to make your money work for you. You'll learn how to create a complete savings, spending, and investing plan that can help you achieve your life goals, feel better financially, and live a happier life. You will find yourself ready—maybe even eager!—to talk to other women about money. And when that happens, we will all lift each other up.

The truth is that money is a tool. Just like a computer or a bicycle, it helps you go places and spend your time in ways you value. Like any tool, you need to keep it in good working order, *and you can.*

So, the first thing I'd like you to do is take a deep breath, sit up straight, and feel a zing of pride. Good for you for taking this first step! And hold that thought about steps. I'll come back to it later.

HOW THIS BOOK UNFOLDS

This book has three sections, and each one builds on the one before it. By the time you come to each new section, you will be well prepared.

Part one is *Believe*.

If you are reading this book, I suspect that at some level you just feel . . . bad about your relationship to money.

- You may be fearful and uncertain about what your financial future holds.
- You may feel disorganized and out of control, but the thought of living differently seems overwhelming.
- You may want to change how you deal with your finances, but you don't know how to find unbiased, clear information or a trustworthy guide.

I have heard all these feelings and more from women all over the United States.

Truly, whatever you're feeling about money right now, you've got company. Often, women who have these feelings seem to internalize their pain. They start to believe that the reason they have a problematic relationship to money is because they have some personal character flaw.

They don't. Please, please believe that.

It is also true that you can be better with money. You can feel more confident, knowledgeable, and focused. That's why you're here, right?! And the first step to being better with money is (drumroll please) believing that you can be.

- When you trust that you are capable of change, you are much more likely to be successful.

- When you feel more self-confident and empowered, that alone will help you make better financial decisions.
- And when you have a clear vision for your future, you will be more likely to make it come true.

You will come away from the Believe section of this book with greater awareness of your money mindset and tools to bolster your self-confidence and self-trust. You will also have greater faith in your ability to change and develop financial knowhow and a clearer vision of the life goals your money can help you achieve.

Part two is *Learn*.

Once your money mindset is empowering and you feel more motivated, you'll be ready to soak up new knowledge and build skills. That is what you will find in this second section.

- You'll learn how to take a snapshot of your financial life.
- You'll learn a clear process for using your money intentionally—and making your intentions stick.
- You'll learn the (jargon-free) basics of becoming an investor.

That may sound like a lot! But I'm going to be with you every step of the way, and I'll share tips and tricks to keep you motivated and moving forward.

While you may feel daunted now, you will see that when you learn to do these things one by one, each will build on what came before it. Imagine building a log cabin, stacking log after log until you have a home to shelter you. Your money skills will grow in the same way.

Part three is *Build*.

By the time you land in this section of the book, you will have made enormous progress developing financial knowledge and skills. Hopefully, you will be feeling better about money as well, with a healthier money mindset and greater confidence.

This third section of the book is where you pull together all that you have learned about yourself and managing your money to create an integrated financial plan that will support you as you reach for your life goals.

- You'll learn how to create a comprehensive goals-based investing plan to provide for your future security—and for your many current priorities.
- You'll integrate your month-to-month spending plan with your investing roadmap to create a set of financial supports that can help you live life on your terms.
- You'll learn how to pay it forward, sharing your new knowledge and skills and supporting the people and causes you love.

All of this sounds good, right? It also sounds like a lot.

In fact, I'm going to guess that if you're not leaning back with your arms crossed and a frown on your face, you're feeling as if you could be. Truthfully, this is a big undertaking. But we are going to break down this whole process into manageable, bite-sized steps, and each one will carry you forward.

HOW TO USE THIS BOOK

Each chapter is divided into three sections: **where we are now,**
what we can do, and **where we go next.**

- **Where we are now** will illuminate the source of your financial stress in this area, and the real reasons why this is not
just something you brought on yourself.
- **What we can do** offers just that: action steps we can take to
feel better. You will be writing, looking up information, and
making plans.
- **Where we go next** will show you how the work you've just
done will lead you forward.

Will you have uncomfortable moments? Yes. But I will be
right there with you. You will finish this book with a clear vision
for your future, the skills and knowledge to make your money
work for you, and an integrated financial plan that will help you
achieve lasting well-being.
You are capable of all this. I am certain of it.

WHY I WROTE THIS BOOK FOR YOU

By now, you may be wondering what makes me think I'm the
person to help you transform your relationship to money. Well,
for starters, I have a passel of credentials to reassure you. I spent
two decades as an award-winning business and financial journalist
at the *New York Times, Business Week*, and CNBC. Before that,
I had a brief stint on Wall Street as a securities analyst. I am also a
trained coach. I know money, and I know how to communicate
about money in a way that is empowering.

But that's just part of the reason I am writing this book. I'm
also doing this because *I have been where you are now.*

The truth is, I made a whole pile of money mistakes after I finished college, thanks in large part to the money story I created for myself growing up.

My father had a privileged upbringing, but in his twenties, he walked away from a lucrative career to become an academic, at which point his parents cut him off financially and their relationship was never the same. My mother was an editor. As parents, if they talked about money at all, it was to teach my brother and me that life choices should not be driven by finances. I also watched my mother get a deer-in-headlights look when it came to anything financial. Not surprisingly, I came to truly dislike thinking about anything money related. The money story I crafted for myself grew out of what I learned from my parents: money brings unhappiness and fights, and I would not be happy if I based life choices on it.

Running on Empty—Really

You can guess what happened when I finished college and got my first job. I rented an apartment that was too expensive and got a car that made no sense—and then struggled from paycheck to paycheck. One morning, sitting at a traffic light waiting to drive downhill to work, I realized I needed to shift my car into neutral so I could coast down that last bit. I was very, very low on gas—and I couldn't buy more until I got paid that afternoon.

No doubt some people would have changed their stripes at that point. Not me. Nor did I change my habits even after attending business school and embarking on a three-year journey to earn a Chartered Financial Analyst, or CFA, investment management certification.

At age thirty, my personal financial life was still messy. I did not track my spending, I did not balance my checkbook, I was—as they say—relaxed about paying certain bills, and I was leery of investing in the stock market. *Even with all my training and know-how, at an emotional level I was still afraid to engage with my money.*

Worse, I felt bad about my money life. I was anxious and ashamed, and I wondered what was wrong with me that I couldn't seem to put my training into practice. But there I was.

My Inadvertent Enlightenment

What changed?

I fell in love, and we got married.

Soon after, we began planning to start a family, and that is when my lightbulb moment came. I realized that if we were going to bring little people into the world, they would need to be fed and clothed and sent to the best schools we could manage, and that was going to require money. I really, really wanted those things to happen. Finally, with my clear, heartfelt goal in mind, I was motivated to put my money to work.

Bit by bit, I began automating my saving, paying bills on time, and investing my savings with a thought-out plan. It sounds simple, and on some level it was. But to make those changes, I first needed a shift in my mindset. Even with my education and training, the internal belief that money was a powerful tool I could capably use was a long time coming.

Losing My Shame

I believed for years that there was something flawed about me that had kept me from getting my finances in good order for so long. But several years ago I shifted my journalistic focus from financial markets and banking to personal finance. That's when I realized my past issues with money were not entirely my fault.

As I researched and reported on story after story about women and their money challenges, I started to see that my own former money habits, and the guilt that followed, were present in a lot of other women too—even women with great educations and lots of personal or professional achievements.

Certainly, women's structural financial challenges were persisting—but so were women's feelings about money. Even millennial women were continuing to cede key long-term financial decisions to their male partners, and many of them believed their partners just naturally knew more.

I started to suspect that the disabling money mindset I knew so well wasn't just a personal issue, but something a lot of women struggled with every day. I also realized I was hungry to know more. I interviewed experts, read research studies, and talked to hundreds of women.

It soon became clear to me that even highly successful women had been fed message upon message about our ability (or inability) to manage money. Many of us had internalized those messages, harming our self-confidence, self-esteem, and sense of self-worth. Women did not become incompetent or flighty. Rather, we lost trust in ourselves and our innate talents. That in turn left us with less internal fortitude to push back when financial challenges inevitably came our way, which left us with more financial stress—and the cycle repeated.

Sharing with You

That is why I decided to start a business focused on empowering women financially, starting with mindsets. I earned an advanced diploma in coaching, and now I layer coaching techniques on top of financial education.

Women who work with me don't just get tips and tricks—they get a new way of thinking about themselves in relation to money. They realize that they truly can take charge of their finances, achieve their goals, and live life on their terms.

With this book, my goal is to help you make that same shift, using techniques I use with my private clients.

But you won't just be hearing from me. In the pages that follow, you will also find the voices of dozens of women with relationships to money that may be very similar to yours. I collected these stories during a two-year project interviewing more than one hundred women about their deepest feelings regarding money.

You will also find the stories of some of my former clients, where they stood when they came to me, and the ways they grew. I am not sharing the real names of any of these women. I have also omitted any identifying details from their stories. But you will hear exactly what they had to say. These brave, generous women are sharing their stories to help you create your own money success.

Trust me. You are worthy, and you are no longer alone with your feelings about money. You can get to a better place with your finances.

WELCOME TO THE CLIMB

That brings me back to my earlier promise about steps.

I encourage you to think of this whole financial-empowerment process as a staircase, with each chapter a step on that flight of stairs. That staircase leads to a door, and behind that door is the future you want—your ideal vision.

As you work your way through this book, you will be progressing on a path toward a better future, using your money as a tool to get you there. You may get winded at times. You may even need to stop and take a breather. That is fine. I have built in much more than money advice at each step on this staircase. You will find tools and suggestions to renew your motivation, keep your goals in focus, and deepen your self-trust.

So, go ahead. When you need to, put the book down. Pause, reflect, and take stock of how far you have come. I'll be waiting for you when you are ready to climb to the next step.

Remember: if you keep your goals—your reasons for change—top of mind, they will act like a lantern shining light on your path to well-being.

The British philosopher Francis Bacon wrote that "All rising to great place is by a winding stair."

That is your mission. Take the first step, and then the next. I'll be cheering you on. We will get you to the top of the staircase, and the future that awaits you through that door.

Chapter One

What's Your Story?

> "When my parents fought, it was only about money. Now, I have 'money is the root of all evil' in my head. I'm not worried about it until I have to be, until I have a problem I have to deal with, and then I get very stressed out."
>
> —Sandy, 30s, marketing professional

> "I've had a lousy money story my whole life, based on the way my parents treated money. They argued about it, and my money story became that money is painful, ignore it, and if you say anything about it, it will get ignored anyway."
>
> —Megan, 50s, coach

> "If you have money you are allowed to do many things, but if you don't you are stuck. Money becomes everything. When I don't have money, I feel like I'm doing something wrong. It's stressful every day of my life."
>
> —Ruby, 50s, teacher

> *"I never seem to get money into my investment account. Every month I think I'll put money in, but I just don't do it. I think I'm worried about an emergency."*
> —Bobbie, 50s, pharmaceutical sales

THE PROMISE

Consciously or not, we all have stories we tell ourselves about money. In this chapter, you'll uncover your own money story and mindset—your first step in developing a more empowered approach to your finances and achieving greater financial well-being.

Please meet a former client of mine who uncovered her own story.

Anne's Story, Part One

Anne grew up with a home life that was unstable, and money was often tight. After her parents' marriage ended, her mother was forced to go to work to support the family. Anne learned to be creative and resourceful because she needed to. That was the state of play that seemed familiar. So, she worked full time while she put herself through college, launched her career, and got married.

On the surface, Anne seemed to have achieved success, even managing to live in a high-cost town with good schools. But to do all that, she was living with little in the way of a financial cushion. Intellectually, she recognized that her situation was precarious, but she self-identified as an intrepid survivor, and she knew her ingenuity had worked for her in the past. She pushed any plans to boost financial stability to the back burner—until a sudden financial emergency upended her life. The family had to downsize, and even with that change, financial security seemed elusive.

WHERE WE ARE NOW

Stories are powerful things, and we humans have used them through the centuries to explain natural phenomena and teach lessons. The ancient Greeks used the story of Persephone to explain the changing seasons. Aesop's fable of the tortoise and the hare demonstrates that slow and steady can win the race.

Not all stories come from the world right around us, though. Some stories we tell ourselves reflect experiences much earlier in our lives, or values and beliefs we developed early on. And sometimes, we outgrow those stories. Sometimes they just don't match our current reality anymore.

For many women, that is especially true when it comes to money.

HOW WE CREATE MONEY STORIES

We form a lot of our ideas about money at an early age. Money plays a big role in family life—not because every family is laser focused on making money, but because it can make so many things possible (or not) for families.

Unlike food or a home, though, money is an abstract concept, and as young children we struggle to understand abstract ideas. As a result, we look to our parents' behavior with money for clues about what to think about financial matters and how we should behave with our own money.

Emily's parents grew up during the Depression and taught her that "we could fall into poverty tomorrow." Now, as an adult, she finds it impossible to relax about her finances. "I'm unable to know how I would live without financial anxiety. To me that means being irresponsible or wasteful."

Emily's experience is not uncommon. As I interviewed women for my research, I asked them where their money beliefs came from. Some 103 of the 109 women I spoke to pointed to their childhoods.

When we live with a story long enough—for our purposes, a story about money—it becomes hardwired in our mind. We don't even consciously summon it up. It just becomes our instinctive, default lens for interpreting and responding to events.

WHEN MONEY STORIES NO LONGER FIT

There is nothing inherently problematic about learning to view the world through a parent's eyes.

Adopting parental money beliefs as children can cause problems, though. (As you saw in the introduction, I have personal experience with this.)

For one thing, young children find it hard to think with nuance. If you have ever heard a young child proclaim that they hate a certain food or they never get to play at a certain park, you know they are thinking in absolutes. Children's money stories can have the same kind of absolutism. But if we are still telling ourselves those stories as adults, they can cause us stress and anxiety. If we believe we will never be able to retire, that is frightening. If we believe we will inevitably spend more than we intend and go over budget, that can lead to self-blame or even keep us from trying to stick to a financial plan.

In addition, parents are only human, and our parents can have less than healthy money beliefs and behaviors. Our parents may have taken the feast-or-famine approach to money, splurging when times were good and having to scrimp when their luck ran out. They may have argued about money. They may have kept us on a tight leash when it came to spending so that we felt bad about the clothes we wore to school. Any of these could have influenced how we feel about money as adults—and how we behave.

The overarching issue is that a child's-eye view of money is almost bound to be one that is not empowered. And if we hang onto that view into adulthood, we may be thinking about money—and about ourselves in relation to our money—in a way that does not reflect all the skills and talents we have developed as adults.

> *"My perception of money is: if I have it, I'm riding super high and if I don't, I'm the lowest of the low. It's tied with my self-image."*
> —Andrea, 40s, administrative assistant

> *"I feel vaguely anxious. I just hope I'm doing the right thing. I don't follow what my investment accounts are doing. I feel like that's an arbitrary pile of money that I can't control. I pay close attention to my checking account. I don't feel completely comfortable."*
> —Agnes, 50s, consultant

The truth is, we outgrow beliefs all the time. If you have ever gone to a high school or college reunion where former classmates remind you of things you did or said that seem totally out of character for you now, you have moved beyond a story. Someone might recall that you used to be the class comedian and you may think, "That's not me!" And it no longer is. Yes, you may have behaved that way in the past—and your former classmates haven't seen you in years, so they haven't seen you change—but that doesn't match who you are today.

If long-ago classmates are out of touch with who we are now, it doesn't really matter. The biggest impact you'll experience will likely be a few embarrassing social media posts. But when we carry around money stories about ourselves that are no longer accurate, or even helpful, that is a problem.

THE REAL DOWNSIDE OF OLD STORIES

Negative, out-of-date money stories can hurt us emotionally as adults. They can affect how we feel about ourselves, which can then affect how we view and act upon the world.

- If our story is that we will never be able to get a handle on our finances, or master a new approach to a financial task, it can reduce our self-confidence.
- A money story that tells us we are just not as good as others at dealing with money makes us feel incompetent and can lower our self-esteem.
- Perhaps we carry a money story that our needs don't deserve the same attention as the needs of others. We are inherently telling ourselves we are not worthy, and that can damage our sense of self-worth.

We can feel bad about how we deal with money even when, by any objective standard, we are capable and successful in our careers, our communities, and our relationships.

Sophia, a former client of mine, came to me because she became highly anxious whenever she needed to work on a budget or tackle other financial tasks. Her tangled-up feelings and anxieties about money even showed up in her body language. She would sit with her legs crossed and arms hugging her sides when she talked about her money. You could feel the stress she was carrying. And this woman, incredibly skilled, intelligent, creative, and courageous, asked me one day after revealing a money fear, "What is wrong with me?"

Nothing was wrong with Sophia. She was professionally accomplished, had a fulfilling family life, and was connected to her community. But she had internalized her money anxieties.

In fact, some of us feel bad about our money lives even when we feel happy and proud about almost everything else we do.

> "When I feel financial stress, typically it shows up initially in feelings of 'I'm so stupid, I can't manage my money.' I feel totally incompetent. Stupid. I should be able to do this better."
>
> —Evie, 52, business owner

The issue extends beyond unpleasant feelings. When we do not feel emotionally solid dealing with money, it gets harder for us to bring our A game to deal with the financial challenges so many of us face. In short, external circumstances affect our internal story, which then affects our external actions.

- We negotiate less often to be paid what we are worth.
- We put our needs behind everyone else's.
- Many of us still cede long-term financial decision-making to others.

A story may just be a story, but an out-of-date money story can affect our well-being.

If the idea of money stories is resonating with you, please know that having a longstanding set of beliefs about money is not a sign of some personal weakness or failing. Whatever happened in the past is over, but it is human nature for experiences to influence our beliefs, especially about abstract things like money.

I am not here to judge you. In fact, I hope you consider this book a judgment-free zone. We are all trying to do the best we can in life, and there is a lot we can't control. Your goal now is to develop the emotional armor and skills you need to use your money in service of your ideal life. That is why we need a money story that reflects who we are today. It should embody not just our past experiences, but also the strengths and talents we deploy in so many other parts of our lives. It needs to give us a complete picture of our past, our present, *and* our potential future.

WHAT WE CAN DO

The first step in creating a money story that reflects our potential is uncovering the money story we are carrying around today.

That may feel a little unsettling. You may never have asked yourself the questions that follow. But if you take your time, dig deep, really notice the story you tell yourself about money, and write it down, it truly will make a difference.

This is a writing exercise, so get some paper or open a document file on your computer.

WHY A WRITING EXERCISE IS YOUR FIRST ACTION ITEM

You may be wondering why the first exercise in this book is not a financial one, like examining your spending habits or making a budget.

You can find plenty of books that make those things your first to-do items. But before you head back to the bookstore, consider this: *if all it took to transform your relationship to money were a spending tracker and a budget, you would have done it already.* You know there are any number of tools for budgeting and tracking spending in libraries and online. You can watch innumerable videos and read hundreds of books about investing.

Even so, here you are—because those resources alone are not enough for you. Until you trust that you are capable of change, and you are truly motivated to make change happen, all the books, videos, and instruction manuals in the world will do little to help you.

Yes, you will find all kinds of clear, actionable suggestions and advice about tracking your spending, creating a budget, and more in the Learn and Build sections of this book. But first, you will find tools and practices to help you see and believe that you truly can do this for yourself. You will see how to build your confidence with money and uncover your true motivation to change. That is where this writing exercise comes in. "Hearing" what you tell yourself about money is your first step to becoming a more confident, capable manager of your finances.

You may decide to tackle the four questions that follow all at once, or you may spend a few minutes on one and return later, again and again. This may be a quick exercise for you if your money feelings are very close to the surface. But there is no one right way for everyone. If you take a while to dig deep with these questions, that will also help you.

Grab a paper and pen and find yourself a quiet place to sit. Take a few deep breaths and relax. Then, ask yourself:

Question One: How do I feel about money?

Truly, there is no one right answer. The point of the first question is for you to notice your go-to, instinctive associations with money.

- Is money something you are comfortable using for your own benefit?

- Does it scare you?
- Do you give it power over you?
- How do you feel when you spend money versus invest your savings?

Remember: How you feel is just . . . how you feel. This has nothing to do with your merits as a person. Honestly *articulating* how you feel about money can simply help you understand the roots of your financial anxiety and discomfort, which in turn will help you start forming a better relationship with money.

Question Two: What does money represent for me?

Again, it is impossible to come up with a wrong answer to this question—but I realize it can still be unsettling. It's quite possible that you have never consciously asked this of yourself. That is fine.

Considering your past experiences with money may highlight what money represents for you today, and how you relate to it. You can give it a try.

However you decide to approach this question, your goal is to really identify without judgment the role that money plays in your life. Remember—no two women are exactly alike.

> "*At this point money represents freedom to me. And because I'm not making enough to cover what I have to pay, it stresses me out a lot. I got myself more in a hole while I was going to school. Now, I have to cancel plans because it's that or put gas in the car.*
>
> —Jerri, 30s, nurse

Question Three: Where do my feelings about money come from?

Many of the women I interviewed for my own research pointed to their upbringing when I asked them this question, but not everyone did. Your response may be entirely different from all of theirs.

Do your best to really flesh out what specifically happened in your past to inform how you feel about money today.

- Where were you when it happened, and how did you feel at the time?
- How much financial education did you receive at home so you could put this experience in context?

The more detailed your answer to this question about money and your personal history, the more it will help you really understand what it is that drove you to pick up this book and take a step toward changing your relationship to money.

> *"I had such a good childhood—but they argued about money. I remember one Christmas my mom crying because my dad had bought her something and she was upset that he spent the money. There was fear. And I feel like I carry that now."*
> —Cassie, 40s, attorney

Question Four: What have I learned to believe about money given the experiences I have had?

Answering this question will show you your money story.

Do your best to just notice what that story is and stay neutral and free of judgment. Your money story is just that: your story. It may not be serving you today—and we're going to address that.

By itself, though, your story is not inherently good or bad. Remember: when you become consciously aware of what you tell yourself as you think about money matters, you get clues as to why you may feel bad about money.

You are on a mission to uncover what is driving your emotions around money so that, ultimately, you can feel better—more capable, confident, and clear. When you discern your money story, write it down.

Congratulations! You've completed the first thought exercise in this book. And you have uncovered a key part of your relationship to money.

Over time, you may well discover that you have more than one money story you tell yourself. You may have a story about money surprises, another about taking charge of your money, and still another about your money future. I suspect, though, that all your money stories will reveal similar things about your identity—about the person you think you are when you are engaging with your finances.

REFLECTIONS

To be clear, I am not suggesting that an updated money story is the solution to all our financial challenges. Millions of women face enormous financial hurdles and contend with financial emergencies that are in no way their fault. The most uplifting money story in the world cannot negate the effects of a job loss or the structural inequities we face.

Still, when we uncover our money story and really start to understand why we relate to money the way we do, it is an essential first step toward financial wellness. Money is so much more than bits of metal and pieces of paper. It carries all kinds of emotional baggage. When that emotional baggage keeps us from living up to our potential, that is a cost that cannot be recouped.

On the flip side, an up-to-date, empowering money story can help us respond confidently and capably when we inevitably encounter financial challenges, large or small. We are better able to bring our knowledge and talents to the task of overcoming what is in front of us.

That is what happened for Anne.

Anne's Story, Part Two

When Anne first came to me, she knew that ingenuity was part of her identity, but she had not noticed how her identity as someone who could get out of scrapes was keeping her in situations where she had to draw on that ability. That in turn was impeding her ability to reach for big goals or draw on her other strengths, like resilience and self-trust. Over time, she realized that she was spending more time and energy on making ends meet than on planning for a future in line with her values and goals.

As Anne learned to tap all her strengths, she saw that if she had a plan for the day-to-day that improved her baseline stability, her creativity and drive could propel her into the future she wanted. She began setting clear goals for herself and her family. Then she started tracking her spending and checking in to make sure it was in line with those goals. Spending time on her finances, she said, was "almost fun." Soon, she started asking to be paid more for freelance work. And later that year, when a new job offer surfaced, she had the self-confidence to stretch and take the role, complete with a higher salary and greater alignment with her long-term career and financial objectives.

WHERE WE GO NEXT

You may not land your dream job after reading this chapter. But you can start creating new, more empowered associations with money. You can rewrite your money story so that it doesn't cause you pain but instead reflects the complete you—including your strengths and potential. You can even rewrite your story to make it one that has you in charge of your finances, a story that sets you on your way toward a healthier relationship with money and greater financial well-being. I will show you how in the next chapter.

You have climbed the first step on the staircase. Well done! Let's keep going, onward and upward.

Chapter Two

Rewrite Your Money Story

"*Rewriting my own story around money is something I'm aware I need to do. I want to not give it the power it has over me.*"
—Riva, 40s, fitness instructor

"*When I feel financially stressed, instead of getting out doing what I need to be doing, I become very low functioning. The lack of money has impacted my life very negatively, though it will never happen again. I'm now doing smart things with my money.*"
—Olivia, 50s, realtor

"*A goal of mine is to try and bring down my financial anxiety. My goal is to live with more freedom around money.*"
—Elise, 60s, financial services professional

> *"I've chosen a profession that doesn't make a lot of money.*
> *Sometimes I hang out with people I grew up with and*
> *they're in very different financial circumstances. Seeing*
> *people younger than me with no financial worries—it's*
> *bizarre and makes me feel bad again."*
>
> —Selena, 30s, social worker

THE PROMISE

You now have a conscious understanding of the money story you are carrying every day, the roots of your current relationship to money. In this chapter, you will learn how to edit and update your story so it can propel you toward greater financial well-being and happiness.

Please meet my former client Karen, who has been down this same road.

Karen's Story, Part One

Karen was married to a wonderful man who always took care of her every need. If she mentioned that she liked a piece of jewelry in a shop window, often, he would go out and buy it for her.

Karen felt cherished and well taken care of—but when her husband died suddenly, she felt like the rug had been pulled out from under her, especially when it came to finances. Her late husband had taken care of everything, from the family finances to the family phones and computers. Karen had not been truly engaged. Now, she was overwhelmed.

WHERE WE ARE NOW

At this point, having uncovered your money story, you may be experiencing conflicting feelings about yourself and your money. On the one hand, you're probably more conscious of what is going on in your mind when the subject of money comes up. You are starting to get a sense that more is possible for you—but at the same time, you are increasingly aware of the money beliefs that stand between where you are now and true well-being.

> *"I have a love-hate relationship with money. I love the independence and the flexibility it brings, and I regret the reliance on it. We go through peaks and valleys with it, and in the valleys, I regret my reliance."*
> —Miranda, 50s, entrepreneur

A former client described the feeling as standing on one side of a bridge that she felt separated her from the community around her. She had trouble seeing how she could make her way across. Sound familiar?

WE ARE LOW ON CONFIDENCE

Confidence is a big deal for many women when it comes to taking charge of our finances. Some 56 percent of women in a 2021 study by Fidelity Investments said they thought their partner was savvier when it came to investing. (Only 34 percent of men said that.)

> *"I don't feel like I'm very knowledgeable about many aspects of financial investments. It's almost like a language I don't speak."*
>
> —Jasmine, 40s, attorney

Confidence can also affect the degree to which we assert ourselves financially. A survey by Lincoln Financial Group found that women were more than twice as likely as men to say they were not familiar with financial planning and investing. (Whether those hyperconfident men are right is another matter—but our feelings on this point are important when it comes to our confidence.)

> *"I gave up exploring my own business until recently. I put my own risk-taking to the side to make sure my husband was always set up. I probably was old-fashioned, putting his career first and mine getting second priority."*
>
> —Erica, 50s, in career transition

There are some early indications that Gen Z women may be developing more confidence with investing and financial planning, a 2021 research report from Bank of America found. But even Gen Z women were still less likely than their male peers to say they feel knowledgeable about investing, managing debt, and saving for retirement. *And when our confidence is low, it can even keep us from using what we do know about managing our money.*

A 2021 study from George Washington University and an international group of collaborators explored why, when men and women are given a test of their financial knowledge, the women score distinctly lower. Only 22 percent of the women in the study correctly answered three questions measuring financial knowledge, compared to 38 percent of the men. But women were much more likely than men to say they did not know the right answer, and when they retook the test without the option to answer "I don't know," roughly a third of the gap in scores went away. The women underestimated themselves.

That is a pretty disempowered situation. And it doesn't have to be that way.

WE ARE MORE CAPABLE THAN WE THINK

The truth is, you know more about money than you think you do.

If that idea sounds familiar, it's because it's close to the opening line of one of the most popular parenting books ever. Way back in 1946, Dr. Benjamin Spock opened his book *Baby and Child Care* with a section called "Trust Yourself" and these words: "You know more than you think you do."

For years, Dr. Spock was widely known as America's foremost "baby doctor." By the time of his death, his book had sold some fifty million copies. Dr. Spock was right about parents—and I believe I'm right about you and your money. I believe you are more than capable of becoming a financially confident, competent woman, and you may already possess the key building blocks you need.

- When you are considering a major purchase like a car, do you automatically compare features and prices to find the best deal financially for you? Comparisons like those are a key money management skill. It's what you would do if you were comparing two mutual funds or stocks you were considering as investments.

- When you talk to your children about school, do you tell them to ignore the subjects they don't like and focus on one, or urge them to do their best in all their classes? Urging your children to stay "invested" in all their classes is just like a basic principle of investing known as diversification. Even if they dislike one class, they may develop a passion for another subject. Similarly, if you diversify and invest in several different stocks, if one loses money, the effect is diluted.
- Perhaps you have a partner and the two of you discuss your spending. Do you weigh what is more important and what is less so? You are distinguishing between needs and wants—an essential part of making sure your spending is aligned with your core values.
- Perhaps you are saving for your own education, or your children's. If so, you have probably researched where to deposit or invest those savings. That means you know how important it is to put your money to work, an integral part of being financially healthy.

In addition, even if we lack confidence in our ability to achieve financial security and ease, many of us are already living in ways that put real-life financial health within reach. As just one example, the number of breadwinners among us has risen steadily over the past few decades. Even after many months of the pandemic, roughly half of mothers are breadwinners among families with children under age eighteen. These mothers contribute on average 40 percent or more of the household's income, according to the Institute for Women's Policy Research.

BETTER THINGS ARE POSSIBLE

What would be possible for us if we knew and believed that we could take charge of our money?

That mental shift would be a game changer. If we believed in our potential, we would be more likely to ask to be paid what we are worth. Women are far less likely than men to negotiate on salary offers, according to both male and female hiring managers. We know negotiating can be treacherous for women, who must learn to walk a fine line between assertiveness and perceived aggression. But deeper confidence would at least enable us to go into salary and hiring negotiations with a greater determination to ask for what we truly deserve.

If we believed we could take charge of our money, we would also reach out to learn how. We would want to learn how to create and use a budget to put our life goals within reach. Yes, we might need more how-to information on budgeting and saving to make this happen, and I will share all that in chapter six. But our motivation to create a spending and savings plan will come from a mindset that says, "I deserve to use my money to achieve my goals and honor my priorities."

Even better, if we believed we could become capable and competent with our finances, we would have a reason to want to learn to invest and make our savings grow—even if the world of investing feels like alien territory right now. (I will teach you investing basics and investing methods in chapters seven and eight.)

When we believe we can achieve financial well-being, we have greater motivation to do the work to get there.

THE SCIENCE OF HOPE

Did that last section leave you skeptical? Are you preparing to dismiss it as happy talk? The truth is that all this material on mindset is rooted in science.

Educational and psychological researchers have spent years studying hope to understand its relationship to motivation and success. The late C. R. Snyder, a psychologist and an expert on hope, defined it as "the perceived capability to derive pathways to desired goals, and motivate oneself via agency thinking to use those pathways." Translation: hope is the ability to discern a pathway to a desired future and the belief that we are capable of getting there.

Hope can motivate and sustain our actions. In the form of an updated, empowering money story, hope can act like a walking stick, helping us up our staircase.

WHAT WE CAN DO

Here are four steps that will help you embed hope and potential in your money story, so it motivates you to achieve financial well-being.

Try to execute on step one all at once. That will open your mind. Then, when you are ready, read through the rest. Give yourself a couple of days for ideas to bubble up. The goal is for you to think broadly about resources and strengths you can use to achieve your financial goals.

When you believe you can achieve a goal and you see a pathway there, that will give you hope. Hope will carry you through all the tools and lessons in the Learn and Build section so you can develop a financial plan that supports your financial well-being.

Step One: Identify your internal resources

Many women tell me they feel alone with their feelings of anxiety and guilt about money, but you have resources you can tap.

- You may have internal strengths you have not considered in the context of money. An online strengths assessment can help here. I have used both the VIA Survey of Character

Strengths and the CliftonStrengths assessment, for myself and with clients. Both surveys will give you an in-depth report for a fee. The VIA survey, found at www.viacharacter.org, also offers a free option.

- These surveys may identify qualities that don't seem to relate to you and money, but think creatively. One strength that surfaced for me was "fairness." The link to money was not obvious—until I realized that fairness relates to financial empowerment and drives me to keep building my business. Thinking about fairness even helped me create a new program to reach a different community of women.
- The qualities that surface for you can become ingredients in your empowered new money story, such as: "I am capable of building a solid business by using my sense of fairness as motivation."

Step Two: Check your language

Do you tell yourself a money story that includes absolute words like "impossible," "never," or "always"? As in, "I will never be able to retire," "Inevitably, I will wind up on the street," or "I always spend more than I should"?

Since a lot of us develop our thoughts about money as children, it's no surprise that we may have absolute words in our stories, just as children do. But we learned in chapter one that in adulthood, absolute words can put a cap on what you frame as achievable for yourself. These words leave you stuck in a place of limited possibility.

See if you can edit your money story to reflect your potential to change. Here are examples to get you thinking.

- "I will never be able to retire" versus "I am getting ready to retire by saving my money and learning to invest it."
- "I always overspend" versus "I am learning how to stick to my spending plan so I can buy a house."

Both stories with possibility acknowledge current financial strain. But both also allow for future positive developments.

Step Three: Try new tools

How have you motivated yourself to make non-financial life changes, like starting an exercise regimen? These methods can help you with your money as well.

For example, a former client of mine was reluctant to examine her spending patterns because she did not want to find out she needed to deprive herself. When I asked her if she had ever successfully accomplished something she thought would involve self-deprivation, she realized she had successfully lost weight on a plan that gave her a whole list of things she could eat. The concept of new food choices kept her motivated—and when I pointed that out, she saw that examining her spending would point her to alternative choices for using her money.

She dove in and reported back that "the more I look at it, the better it feels." She also realized she could craft a story that linked watching her spending to creating choices and achieving financial well-being.

Don't be afraid to think creatively about tools you can use. A former neighbor of mine struggled to save money because she did not have a specific reason or motivation. Then she hung a bathing suit in her refrigerator to remind her of potential future vacations. (This is true.) It kept her focused, and she started making day-to-day spending choices that gave her the savings to pay for a trip.

To be clear, I am not suggesting swimsuits as a standard part of your personal finance toolkit! The idea is just to think broadly about your past successes. Whatever has worked for you in the past could potentially help you change your money mindset and stick to your goals. (But of course, if a bikini in your produce drawer induces you to save more, go for it. Remember—this is a judgment-free zone.)

Step Four: Write your new story

Here is your moment. Take the money story you identified in chapter one and write it down on paper. Next, reframe it to include the potential for a better future.

Say your story is that a financial disaster could be right around the corner at any time. You may truly believe that— but you don't have to assume you will face it unprepared. Let's imagine that you identified a strength like gratitude. And let's say you noticed you are more successful when you map out a step-by-step plan toward a goal.

Your new money story could be something like, "I am building my emergency fund with every paycheck (that's the step-by-step part), and I will reward myself monthly for my achievement (gratitude), so so if financial disaster strikes, I will be ready." That's a little more empowering, right?

REFLECTIONS

You will know that you have landed on your accurate money story when you read it and think *YES*. Your updated, empowering money story may even make you smile. Ideally, it will also make you feel ready to act. You may not have been paying a lot of conscious attention to your finances in the past, for any number of reasons, but money is a key tool you can use to achieve your goals and live life on your terms once you get your financial life in order.

You will need to get your hands a little dirty to make this happen. But I will help you and show you how. Remember: as Dr. Spock said (in a very different context, but still), you know more than you think you do.

Karen, for one, found that she was able to do more than she expected.

Karen's Story, Part Two

While Karen may have felt helpless after her husband died, the truth is, she was anything but. As an independent woman newly on her own, she mastered all kinds of new skills she needed to run her household. Karen's husband had always handled their computers and other home technology, for example. But at one point, her printer stopped working and Karen managed to resolve the issue on her own.

The feeling of empowerment she got from that spurred her to tackle all kinds of things she had left to her late husband, from choosing a better cell phone plan to hiring a financial advisor she liked and trusted.

As we examined her growing confidence, Karen realized that she could also lose her old feelings of helplessness about money. She realized she was capable of developing new skills. "I can be uncomfortable, and I can handle it. It will be okay," she realized.

That mindset—that revised story—empowered Karen to really look at where her money was going. She said she wanted to stop feeling anxious about running out of savings, and she realized that she could make that happen if she started looking at what was happening with her money day-to-day.

Lo and behold, Karen found that she had been spending much more than she thought on pastimes that were enjoyable but not very fulfilling. She quickly made changes and her cash flow improved. That shift allowed her to pay for music lessons, something she had long wanted to do. A year later, her financial anxiety is still a thing of the past, and her music making is bringing her joy.

WHERE WE GO NEXT

Just like Karen, you are now the proud owner of a money story that reflects your true potential and the strengths you bring to a task. Congratulations! You just rose a step higher on our staircase. It is now time to put your money story to use to improve your everyday life. That is what we will work on next.

Chapter Three

Rewrite Your
Money Relationships

> "*My biggest money challenge is communication with my husband. He has a philosophy that's different from mine. His is 'it's always worked out, it always will, don't worry.' Mine is 'it's always worked out because we've had a plan.'*"
>
> —Charlotte, 50s, marketing executive

> "*Honestly, I let my husband handle all our finances and I turn over my check. I feel like I have zero independent knowledge, so money can be very nerve-wracking. I'll spend and then there is an argument.*"
>
> —Alexis, 40s, attorney

"We had gotten ourselves into a lot of debt. I worked my butt off, and I got us out of about $20,000 in debt. And that month I opened the bill to a $4,000 charge where my husband bought a sports car. That precipitated my divorce. It was a wake-up call for me to take control."

—Prisha, 50s, business owner

"I've been married twice, and I have always out-earned my spouse by at least double. It's nerve-wracking because if I were to lose my job, I feel responsible for the well-being of my family. I also think it represents a point of envy for my husband."

—Janet, 40s, manufacturing executive

THE PROMISE

Money is one of the biggest sources of conflict in our relationships, and we will explore why that is. In this chapter, you will also learn how the strengths and potential underlying your new money story can help you approach the financial part of your relationship with greater confidence and an eye on your financial well-being.

The story of Paula, one of my former clients, is an example.

Paula's Story, Part One

Paula is a driven, high-achieving woman who works hard and lives well. She came to me, she said, because she wanted to get a handle on her financial future. She was highly confident that she and her husband could both earn what they needed to support the life they wanted—but the two of them had not mapped out a plan for their next chapter. They also did not have a set plan regarding paying for college for their three children.

Initially, Paula believed she could sort out her own financial issues with me and keep her relationship out of the picture. Their finances were mostly separate, other than an account for household expenses, and part of Paula's identity was that she was a strong survivor and could take care of herself.

It soon became clear, though, that Paula's money issues had a lot to do with her spouse. She was unhappy with their lack of communication about money matters, and she resented that he did not share the details of his finances, nor those of his business. She found it hard to think about planning for the future without having a full understanding of where they both stood financially. She also said that he liked to live on very little, and he regularly became angry with her about her spending, which she said was mostly for their children. Sometimes, she hid purchases from him.

WHERE WE ARE NOW

If you were to list the top stressors on your relationship with your spouse or longtime partner, what would you say? Sex is high on many people's lists. Childrearing can also cause tension and discord. And then there is money. Money and finances are among the most common causes of friction in relationships. Nearly seven in ten people who are married or living together have had a money-related dispute with their partner in the past year, according to a survey by the American Institute of CPAs. Twenty-six percent say money issues are a source of tension at least once a month.

Money is, in fact, one of the most often cited causes of divorce. Various studies over the past several years have found that financial issues were a major reason couples ended their marriages. (And who usually winds up losing financially after divorce? You guessed it. Women.)

Apart from divorce, financial infidelity—the deliberate concealment of financial information or a purchase, or outright lying about money matters—is present in more than 40 percent of relationships where couples pool their finances, according to the National Endowment for Financial Education.

WHERE THE TENSION STARTS

How did we get here? The saying "love is blind" has some truth to it, evidently. It is very common for couples to start combining their finances before having an in-depth conversation about their money histories and values.

A 2019 survey by SunTrust (now Truist) found that while 88 percent of couples say they believe a premarital money conversation is important, when it comes to real life, only 51 percent of couples have that conversation before tying the knot. Just four in ten disclose their salaries to each other, and only a third talk about their respective debt. (Happily, there is more disclosure among younger couples, but the numbers are still low.)

In addition, we each bring our own unique histories with money to our relationships, along with our notions of how to behave financially day-to-day. People who grew up in a home where money was scarce may savor the short-term pleasure a small splurge can provide, but people who were raised to focus hard on long-term goals may be exasperated and even frightened by that kind of spending. One of you may really like having a financial plan, while the other may have learned to be comfortable winging it. Same-sex couples may have slightly different financial stressors, according to Stuart Armstrong, a Certified Financial Planner (CFP) with Centinel Financial Group.

"I think a lot of couples when they were considered legal strangers never got around to doing the things they should have been doing," he said. "That probably created different kinds of stress and anxiety, increasing the lack of preparedness."

If we don't discuss these things early (and often), they can become a source of increasing frustration for both parties.

> *"Money creates conflict with my husband. He is a spender, and I am not. I'm very cautious about spending. A $100 expense makes me crazy."*
>
> —Nadine, 30s, pharmaceutical sales representative

> *"When I am under financial stress I usually scream and yell. Usually, it's directed at my husband, and it's 'why did you spend money on this or that.' I don't get high blood pressure. I give it."*
>
> —Blaire, 40s, entrepreneur

Relationship stress due to finances can also build up over time. The money priorities a couple sets can gradually breed resentment, for example. Many women have told me that they put their own needs behind everyone else's in the family, to the detriment of their career development or their businesses.

> *"I feel a lot of stress when I am spending money either for myself or for something work-related that is for me. We're at the bottom of the totem pole."*
>
> —Heather, 50s, media executive

Another long-term problem can develop when, as often happens, one partner takes the lead on managing shared finances. Both partners may happily decide early on who should be primarily in charge of financial tasks and planning. Over time, though, communication about finances can suffer, and the less-involved partner can start to feel out of the loop. That in turn can breed resentment.

> *"I have an education, I'm pretty good in math and understanding numbers. But I can't wrap my head around financial concepts. My husband does all the investing, and when I ask him about it, he gets very defensive. And I say, 'That's garbage—you want me to be an independent woman, but you won't explain.' At one point I was ready to end the marriage, and it opened my eyes a lot to—where is the money and how could I just walk out? I'm still here. I think I'm married because of the finances."*
> —Sara, 40s, health care professional

A Fidelity Investments survey found that fewer than six in ten respondents make long-term financial decisions jointly with their partner. Roughly four in ten could not say how much their partner earns.

In the past, relative income has influenced who takes the lead on financial decisions and long-term financial planning, more often the higher earning partner, according to a study by the Federal Reserve Bank of Boston. Long term, that's a potential positive for women, since more of us are becoming major breadwinners. But so far, the increase in breadwinning has not occurred evenly across the income spectrum. Mothers in the lowest income quintile are far more likely to be sole or primary breadwinners than mothers in the top quintile.

In higher-income families, men tend to be the long-term financial decision-makers. In a survey of high net worth couples' money habits by the multinational bank UBS, 69 percent of men said they took the lead, and only 20 percent of couples made long-term financial decisions together.

Then there is the matter of self-worth. Some people's sense of their own worth is highly contingent on the state of their finances. These people are more likely to use negative, emotion-laden words when they talk about financial stressors. They are also more apt to report that they argue with their partner about finances, according to Lora Park, an associate professor at the University of Buffalo, SUNY.

THE COST OF FINANCIAL RELATIONSHIP STRAIN

Pull that all together, and it seems that suboptimal communication and slow-brewing tensions affect many couples' financial lives together—and their relationships in general. That is problematic in several ways, even apart from the sobering divorce statistics I shared at the beginning of the chapter.

For one thing, life brings surprises, like job loss and sudden illness. If we are not in sync in terms of our finances, one or both partners can experience enormous stress if disaster strikes.

> *"When my husband lost his job, I had a feeling that I didn't dare slow down. I went straight to the disaster scenario. I'd wake up at night having panic attacks and wake up in the morning feeling enraged. We went through my savings cushion very quickly and that broke my heart."*
> —Maeve, 40s, editor

Money tensions in a relationship can also reduce our overall relationship satisfaction, according to numerous studies. On a personal level, financial tensions can lower our self-confidence and sense of self-worth, which in turn can impede our ability to achieve well-being, financially and otherwise.

> *"I feel fairly confident financially. I feel that faltering a little when I talk to my husband and say, 'Show me what you're doing' and he says, 'Well, you don't really have the background to understand.'"*
>
> —Margaret, 50s, business owner

IT CAN BE BETTER

On the flip side, when we are on the same page as our partner on money matters, it can feed our confidence and our relationship satisfaction. That, in turn, can keep us motivated to become more empowered and capable with money.

WHAT WE CAN DO

The suggestions that follow are intended to help anyone in a long-term relationship get to a happier money life.

Step One: Consider the past

In the last two chapters, you uncovered your own history with money, and you probably discovered things that you had not realized were affecting your behavior today. You can't force your partner to go through that same process, but on your own, you can reflect on where their beliefs about money originated. This is unlikely to change any feeling that the two of you are operating from different scripts—but if you consciously think about this, you may at least feel like your partner isn't completely irrational. Just like you, their past is informing their present.

To be sure, unless you are planning to end your relationship, your partner's money behavior is going to be an element in your life together. But you don't have to just grin and bear it. Together, you can find ways to honor both of your approaches.

For example, let's say one of you feels insecure unless you are saving as much money as humanly possible, and the other feels that life is to be enjoyed and extra cash is an opportunity to have some fun right now. You can both decide that each of you will get an equal amount of money every month to use as you wish—an amount small enough to keep your overall financial life intact, but something. The saver can put away their half of the money for the future, and the spender can use theirs however they like. The saver winds up feeling safe, and the spender gets to enjoy spending without reproach.

Note: Setting up a system like this will work better if you have a budget, or as I like to call it, a statement of intent. I'll cover budgeting in detail in chapter six.

Step Two: Be aware of the present

Even with the best intentions, we can quickly grow angry if it feels like we are not working from the same financial playbook as our partner. Often, those feelings arise when we find out about a partner's financial activity after the fact.

When one partner takes the lead on financial tasks and decision-making, it can work just fine. But staying engaged is key. If you check out of that part of your life together, your feeling of being out of sync with your partner can be especially acute.

For the health of your relationship—and your own well-being—you need to maintain some awareness of what is going on with you both financially. That means making sure both of you have access to all your relevant accounts. It is much, much easier to have a conversation about what's going on when you both have equal access to information.

Younger couples are especially likely to maintain at least some financial separation, and that is fine. Whether or not you combine your finances, you just need to be able to see what is going on in any account whose balance can affect how you live.

You may find surprises, especially if you have not focused on your finances in the past. You may not have realized what your partner—or you—were spending on a favorite hobby or how little your financial cushion really is. Do your best to stay neutral and calm in that moment. You are gathering information so you can plan more effectively going forward.

If you and your partner work with a financial advisor, make sure the lines of communication for both of you are open there too. (I'll say more about financial advisors in chapter eight. For now I will just say that with the right qualifications, they can be extremely helpful, and you don't have to be wealthy to have one.) The more comfortable you are talking to your financial advisor, the more prepared that person will be to support you if you need it. The same will be true for your spouse.

Step Three: Keep it up

Are you committed to reflecting on the source of your partner's money beliefs? Are you making sure that both of you have full access to all the financial accounts that can affect you? Congratulations!

But this is not a one-and-done thing. Money is a constant in our lives, like it or not. We need to stay on top of our finances, even if we are not the primary financial decision-maker or bill payer. At least once a month, give yourself thirty minutes or an hour to go over your joint spending. Look over your Venmo account, your bank statements, your credit card spending, and see where your money is going. Even if your partner is not open to this, you can do it yourself. It's even better if your partner wants to do it with you.

Please don't think I have everything figured out about relationships. Far from it! But my husband and I do have a system for ongoing financial communication. As you probably guessed, I take the day-to-day lead on money tasks and planning in my family. But every month, my husband and I have regular money catchups to go over what is happening with us financially. We review ongoing spending and anticipated expenses, check in on our savings and investments, and go over credit card and bank statements to make sure everything is in order.

When we have financial to-do items like filing health insurance claims or looking into refinancing our mortgage, we split that list and each take some. Our reward comes when we get to think about how to use any free cash that is not allocated for savings or expenses. We might discuss travel or an activity with our kids, and it's a great way to finish these catch-ups smiling. You can try something similar.

REFLECTIONS

It is highly unlikely that you and your partner will have identical relationships with money. But then again, you probably have different feelings about a lot of things, from food, to music, to your favorite way to spend a Sunday afternoon. If we can manage to work out those differences, we can do the same with money.

Even better, when we can enter a money discussion with a feeling that we deserve to be on equal footing, we can better open ourselves to learning new approaches to financial tasks. We can teach our partners a few things too. Money harmony can strengthen a relationship well beyond the dollars and cents.

That is what Paula found when she initiated a money talk.

Paula's Story, Part Two

When Paula first came to me, she knew she wanted a clearer plan for her financial future. She also knew she wanted to be with her husband long term, but their disagreements over money matters were keeping her from achieving either goal. Their arguments were a source of stress for her.

As we worked together, Paula saw that she had the power to initiate the change she wanted. She also saw that her secret spending was not in line with the strong woman she knew herself to be. We talked about how she could bring her internal strength to having an open, honest conversation with her husband about their financial issues.

That is what she did, and she reported that it was transformational for their relationship, almost as if they stripped away all the secrets between them. That success also emboldened her financially. She started devouring financial information and educating herself, and she and her husband started having regular money conversations and sharing ideas.

WHERE WE GO NEXT

Are you feeling a bit winded? This particular step on the staircase can seem very steep. Give yourself a pat on the back. If you've gotten this far, you've already accomplished a lot on your way to financial wellness. Great job!

Are you feeling better than you did on page one? That's terrific. Are you feeling like you want to set some goals and start learning how to get there? You are in the right place. That is exactly what we will do in chapter four.

Chapter Four

Uncover Your "Why"

"The next chapter is the source of the fear. I need to feel secure. I don't like not knowing that there is this pile over here. I don't know how much we are going to need. My husband doesn't plan on retiring. But I feel like we need a number. Something we are shooting for. And how much we will have to live on per year for however long that is."

—Janice, 50s, author

"Right now, my concern is what am I going to do when my husband isn't here? Something is coming down the road and I don't know when it will be or how to handle it. I want to build financial competency and get my daughters to a place of capability."

—Gerri, 50s, former attorney

THE PROMISE

It is easy to spend our time caught up in day-to-day thoughts, financial and otherwise. When we articulate our heartfelt life goals, as we will in this chapter, we gain energy and focus. That in turn gives us motivation to develop the skills and practices that will help us succeed.

Eileen's story is a case in point.

Eileen's Story, Part One

Eileen, a successful business owner with a very full life, had worked hard to achieve professional success. She was happy with a work-life balance that netted her an income she was proud of and quality time with her family. In fact, she said her day-to-day life, while hectic, was very satisfying.

When it came to long-term goals, though, Eileen felt nervous. She knew she did not want to work indefinitely, but she worried about achieving the financial security that would enable her to retire. She and her husband also found it hard to make big financial choices because they lacked clarity about their next chapter. They would spend hours going back and forth before choosing a new car or planning a vacation, and that made her anxious. In addition, when it came to long-term financial decisions, she felt very much at sea. She lacked a plan for moving forward.

WHERE WE ARE NOW:
CONSUMED BY THE DAY-TO-DAY

In her book *The Writing Life*, Annie Dillard wrote that "how we spend our days is, of course, how we spend our lives." Very true! And in an ideal world, we would unspool our days in ways that fulfill us now *and* put our long-term goals in reach. Unfortunately, modern life does not leave us a lot of room for sitting quietly and articulating long-term goals—financial or otherwise. Many of us are wearing multiple hats over the course of a week—or a day.

Women regularly contend with the so-called second shift, all the unpaid labor we perform at home caring for children and family after our paid work is over for the day. Raising children has become a more demanding job in the past fifty years, with moms spending fourteen hours a week on childcare in 2016, up from ten in 1965, according to the Pew Research Center. (Of course, that increase has taken place even as millions more women entered the workforce, and women's hours per week at work nearly tripled.) Men have taken on a larger share of the housework, but large-scale surveys measuring how Americans use time show that women still perform 50 percent more.

CARRYING THE MENTAL LOAD

Women are also more likely to carry the mental load of family life. We tend to be the ones anticipating tasks that need to be organized and monitoring children's social, emotional, and educational lives. All of this was driven home in graphic terms during the pandemic, when millions of women found themselves taking the lead on overseeing their children's remote schooling on top of their regular jobs.

Even when children can be dropped off at school, that mental load is present. A 2017 report by Bright Horizons, the largest provider of employer-sponsored childcare, rattled off numerous examples of the odds and ends on many mothers' minds, from carpools, doctor's appointments, science fairs, and play dates.

It's not just mothers, though. With or without children, women juggle responsibilities every day. We have challenging lives, and for the most part we do a great job of meeting those challenges. But it's still a lot.

UNSETTLED ABOUT THE FUTURE

In addition to being busy, many women find it uncomfortable to think about big lifetime goals because they are just not sure that financially, those goals are attainable. The gender pay gap is a major cause of that unease. Women on average earn just 82 cents for every dollar men earn, and most women of color earn much less. That gap has barely changed in twenty years, and it has a ripple effect throughout women's lives. It takes women roughly two years longer to repay student loans, and women have less money they can save for retirement. A prepandemic study prepared for the Asset Funders Network estimated that single women reach retirement facing a yawning wealth gap, owning just 32 cents for every dollar a single man owned, and the pandemic has done nothing to help matters, with more women than men losing their jobs or exiting the workforce.

Not surprisingly, nearly four in five American women said in a 2021 study that they felt weighed down by finances. And 40 percent of the women in a Capital Group survey said they expected the pandemic to have a long-term effect on their financial lives.

STUCK ON "SPIN CYCLE"

I hope you are starting to see how all of this discourages us from stepping back and visualizing our ideal next chapter. Between our busy days and our sense of financial unease, the last thing many of us want to do is wade into planning mode. But that can leave us with a financial life that feels like a washing machine stuck on spin cycle: we do what we need to do to get through the day, worry vaguely from time to time about whether we are doing what we need to be doing for our future, and quickly become uncomfortable enough that we are only too happy to turn back to immediate concerns . . . to the detriment of our long-term financial security.

BENEFITS OF SETTING GOALS

Think back to what Annie Dillard said about how we spend our days. Wouldn't it be nice to know as we move through our days that we are progressing bit by bit toward the future we want?

We can do that—with our finances. In fact, an awful lot of financial advice boils down to something like, "make this small move, and do it on repeat." The problem is that this process can become demoralizing very quickly if we don't have a sense of what those moves will make possible for us.

That is why an ambitious, heartfelt goal can make all the difference. When we articulate big challenging goals, we gain focus. Instead of feeling mired in the day-to-day, we have a direction we want to go.

Your big goals may have to do with feelings as much as with achievements. In fact, if you think about it, the true intrinsic outcome we seek from achievement-based goals is often a feeling.

When I interviewed women about their money lives, I asked them to describe what it would feel like to achieve financial ease.

No one mentioned greater status or pointed to things their new wealth could buy them. Their answers seemed to come straight from the heart:

> "I would feel better about myself."
> "I would feel a general calm."
> "It would give me some hope."
> "It would feel like an enormous burden was lifted."
> "I could feel like I was living instead of just existing."

A big long-term goal can motivate us to take the short-term steps that will help us achieve it. The goal also gives us a way to gauge our progress so we can be proud of our success along the way.

It's not just me saying this. Experts in behavioral psychology have studied the types of motivation that yield the greatest, most lasting success. They analyzed the types of motivation driving cadets at West Point—a motivated bunch—and measured how cadets with different motives fared. Cadets with strong, solely internal motives to succeed were more likely to graduate and become commissioned officers. Longer term, they were also more likely to receive early recommendations for promotions.

There is another benefit to setting big ambitious goals: it turns out that we are happiest when we are chipping away at a big challenging personal objective.

Consider the findings of Tal Ben-Shahar, an expert on positive psychology and leadership and the creator of a wildly popular course on happiness at Harvard University. "Attaining lasting happiness requires that we enjoy the journey on our way toward a destination we deem valuable," he wrote in his bestselling book *Happier.* "Happiness is not about making it to the peak of the mountain nor is it about climbing aimlessly around the mountain; happiness is the experience of climbing toward the peak."

WHAT WE CAN DO

I'm going to share several coaching exercises I have used with clients to help you identify goals that can move you forward. Please, take your time completing these and dig deep. Write down what you come up with on the worksheet in the appendix and add as much detail as you can. No one will ever need to see this besides you, so be bold and go where your imagination takes you.

Do your best to flesh out your vision of your ideal future as much as possible. More detailed goals give you greater focus and motivation, so the less haze the better. One other thing: You may come up with goals that feel unattainable. If the specifics seem improbable—not all of us can become soloists with American Ballet Theatre (ABT)—consider the elements making that goal compelling for you. How would you feel if you achieved that goal? What would achieving that goal make possible for you? *Those outcomes may be your true goal—and they may be achievable in more ways than one.* ABT may be out of reach, but you can still dance, take pride in your strength and grace, and share your art with the world.

Step One: Imagine your ideal future

Close your eyes and imagine that it is five or ten years from now, and that in the time between now and then, everything has gone exactly the way you wanted it to. Anytime a situation could turn out badly or well for you, it turned out well. In this imagined future, you are living your ideal life.

Now, ask yourself:

- Where are you? Do your best to articulate exactly what your surroundings look and feel like.
- Who are you with? Are you working with colleagues you admire? Spending time with people you love? Again, the more detail the better.
- How are you spending your days?

Note that this future does not need to be extravagant. It certainly does not have to have anything to do with money. It just needs to be the future you most want for yourself.

> *"I would like to start a family in the next few years. I'm also interested in fostering kids. I want to write another book, and I want to grow my business and become THE authority in my field."*
>
> —Christie, 30s, entrepreneur
>
> *"I want to go to nursing school. And I want to have enough money for vacations."*
>
> —Maya, 30s, marketing professional
>
> *"This job eats up my world and I don't want to leave this earth knowing this was all I did. I'd like to maybe work for a nonprofit, give back to the community."*
>
> —Rhonda, 50s, manager

Step Two: Imagine your retirement party

This exercise takes the opposite approach to identifying your goals. Summon up a vision of what your future retirement party could look like. You know you will have family and colleagues cheering for you, and chances are, you will be asked to share a few thoughts.

Now, imagine that a younger colleague asks you, "What do you regret not having done?"

Do your best to be nonjudgmental with yourself as you think about your response. You may come up with travel plans you deferred, an academic degree you were not able to pursue . . . anything (legal) is fair game.

Next, flip that list around. In an ideal future, would you include those things now? Plenty of people go back to school late in life, for example. You can use the items on this list to flesh out the vision of your ideal future that you identified in Step One.

> *"I wanted to spend a year abroad and we never did. We had children and my husband had a company. Now I'm thinking, what would be the harm in just going for a month? I haven't given up on it!"*
> —Moira, 50s, financial services professional

Step Three: Your perfect ordinary day

Have you ever imagined what you might do if you won the lottery or found a million-dollar bill on the sidewalk? (I'm raising my hand right now.) These daydreams can be fun, but what will help you more with goal-setting is to think about what you really want in a typical day. The idea is to imagine a day that you would be happy to have on repeat.

Again, this does not need to be a fancy twenty-four hours. You might crave a daily hour with a good book or a walk in a park with your spouse. Your task is to fill in the details of what you want most in your everyday life.

> *"I do love to cook. And I want time bonding with my kids, exercising, time to really chat with my husband, and intellectually challenging work. Bonding with your kids doesn't have to be complicated. Connecting with your husband doesn't have to be over a fancy dinner."*
> —Amelia, 40s, consumer products manager

Some of my clients have found it helpful to choose a physical reminder of their goal that they can carry with them. One client began carrying a pebble from a beach she loved to remind her of her goal of having a house by the water. Another made her computer screen saver an image that brought her goal to mind.

REFLECTIONS

You may find one of these exercises especially helpful, and another may leave you cold. That is fine. Use whatever helps you visualize the future you want. The idea is to finish these with a detailed vision of your biggest, most heartfelt life goals.

My former client Eileen found the best-life exercise especially eye-opening.

Eileen's Story, Part Two

When Eileen came to me, she was having difficulty saving for the future and unsure how much she needed to put away. She intended to add to an investment account every month, but when we met it was early autumn and she had not done so that year.

Eileen said she wanted a financial plan, but she had a busy life day-to-day, and she was afraid of learning to invest, even though she knew that would have to be part of any plan. Her big insight came when she realized that if she could stop spending so much time on financial decisions, she could devote that time to things that were more rewarding, like time with her kids and a favorite hobby. She also realized that if she could start feeling financially stable and secure, she could make a long-held personal charitable goal come true.

Two weeks later, Eileen and her husband had reviewed all their joint accounts and set an intention to review their finances every quarter. They had also discussed when they both wanted to retire.

"It felt . . . good," she reported.

WHERE WE GO NEXT

You deserve to feel good too. You have taken big steps toward the financial future you want.

Already, you have climbed up several steep steps, uncovering and rewriting your money story, adjusting how you relate financially to the people you love, and now setting yourself a big ambitious goal to strive for.

We have not yet specifically discussed money-management skills. That comes next, and you will start the upcoming section having completed the essential mental and emotional groundwork to put success within reach.

Remember what I told you early on: if all you needed to get your money life in order were tips and tricks, you would have achieved financial wellness long ago. I know from my research and my experience with clients that the "heart" part of the path to financial well-being is every bit as important as the "head" part. Good for you for sticking with it and getting it done.

Now, it's time to shift gears. The next section of the book, Learn, is chock full of financial information and tools to get you on the road to success.

We will start by taking a snapshot of where you are today. Then we will draw a detailed map to get you where you want to go.

Let's get this moving!

Chapter Five

Take a Snapshot

"*I work very hard to have money and to accumulate it. But twenty years in and I'm like, when is enough enough? There's no end to enough. Life is good. I can't complain. But I do struggle with how money is an all-encompassing part of my life.*"

—Rebecca, 40s, financial services professional

"*Money represents do you keep your house? Do you pay for your kid's health? Your own health care? I don't even think that much about retirement. My savings have been blown through with health insurance.*"

—Clara, 60s, journalist

"*When I look back at people like my grandparents, with one parent at home at least for a while, and to be able to be middle class . . . that now seems obscene to me, what you would have to make these days to make that happen.*"

—Roberta, 40s, content marketing manager

THE PROMISE

Our financial lives can be multilayered, and with everything else we have going on in our lives, it can be hard to stay on top of what is happening with our money. But without that clarity, it is hard to formulate a plan to get where we want to be financially in the future. In this chapter, you will learn how to examine where you stand today, an essential first step in making a financial plan to achieve your goals.

Patricia learned this on short notice.

Patricia's Story, Part One

Patricia, a highly intelligent consultant with a very full life, was the primary (but not the sole) breadwinner for her family. While their lives were not fancy, there was financial stability. But when her husband experienced a life-threatening injury and was unable to work, everything was thrown off.

Patricia was rightly confident about her professional skills, but the family emergency drove home the fragility of their financial situation. They had been putting money away for retirement, but they had not saved a lot for their teenage children's college tuitions and their emergency fund was getting depleted. Patricia worried about how long the family could manage in their current situation if her husband could not return to work.

WHERE WE ARE NOW:
FLYING THROUGH CLOUDS

Many women reach middle age and look around, wondering why we don't feel better financially. Only 47 percent of the women in a Bank of America Merrill Lynch survey rated their financial security as good or excellent, compared to 57 percent of men, and women were twice as likely as men to say financial stress kept them up at night (11 percent versus 5 percent).

Women are also more likely than men to live paycheck to paycheck, and to have less of a financial cushion. Some 47 percent of women could not easily handle a sudden $400 expense, compared to 35 percent of men, according to a BlackRock survey.

In my own research, when I asked women about their most immediate money challenges, making ends meet and having the ability to save more topped the list for all age groups. More than half of the one hundred–plus women I interviewed cited one or both of these challenges as their biggest financial stressor.

> "We look and think okay, we've saved a lot—but also it's not even close to enough. We are uncertain if we have enough."
>
> —Eleanor, 40s, business owner

There are plenty of structural reasons why this is the case, from the gender pay gap, to all the time women spend out of the workforce, and more. Many of us also see our earnings peak well before our expenses do. On average, women hit our top earning years in our early forties, a decade younger than men. In midlife, we also start to experience age discrimination in the workplace, and in job hunting. But at the same time, we may still be dealing with financial challenges like saving for ever-more-expensive college educations for our children.

> *"Money is very worrisome and stresses me out horrifically. It keeps me up many nights. Every time you think you have a handle on something, the rug gets pulled out from under you. My husband lost his job, and we are set up for two incomes. Now my biggest challenge is making ends meet on a monthly basis."*
>
> —Cokie, 40s, business unit manager

Divorce also makes it harder for many women to achieve financial wellness and make it from one paycheck to the next. Divorce rates are declining among millennials, but so-called gray divorce—divorce after age 50—is nearly twice as common as it was in 1990, and women tend to experience more negative financial effects when a marriage ends.

All of these are obstacles, no question. But there is more to the picture.

WE DON'T WANT TO LOOK

Many, many women are ambivalent about the prospect of getting a clear handle on where they stand financially. Only 17 percent of women frequently discuss topics like saving, investing, and retirement planning with family or friends, according to a survey by the Transamerica Center for Retirement Studies—and 28 percent never do. In that same survey, researchers asked both men and women to estimate how much they would need in savings for retirement. Some 52 percent of the women guessed, compared to just 37 percent of the men.

There are indications that the economic upheaval wrought by the pandemic is leading some women to pay more attention to their finances.

But there are still many women who decide the best stress response is just to ignore the whole money part of their lives. (That would be me, around age twenty-two.) If we look the other way, our finances can't hurt us, right?

> *"I don't want to talk about money. I want to act like it doesn't exist."*
>
> —Karin, 40s, public relations professional

When we don't look, though, we are left with ongoing uncertainty, which creates its own kind of anxiety.

> *"I think about where I can pull from to pay a big bill. I wonder, 'Uh oh, is this sustainable?'*
>
> *My financial plan got shredded by my divorce. Now I don't have the plan."*
>
> —Meghan, 40s, business owner

One former client of mine was deeply averse to taking a hard look at her finances. But that meant that every time she went to an ATM to take out cash, she would say a little prayer in hopes that there would be money she could withdraw.

> *"I hate tending to my finances. I pay bills late because I hate doing it so much. The money can be there, but I think it stems from not having money in the past. It's created this whole anxiety thing within me. I get physically ill from paying bills."*
>
> —Enid, 50s, human resources manager

The problem with not knowing—in addition to uncertainty and anxiety—is that it puts coherent financial planning out of reach. Women have told me they just don't know if they are saving the "right" amount or if their savings target is "reasonable."

We don't have the knowledge or the facts we need to develop a well-informed view of our money lives. As a result, we can wind up depriving ourselves unnecessarily, or on the flip side, spending too much of our hard-earned money on things that are not truly important to us, leaving us short on funds for essentials.

OPENING OUR EYES

The truth is, there is a simple first step we can take to change all this: we can take a good look at where we stand financially. That way, we can start to see any changes we need to make in our money lives to feel better financially.

Now you may be thinking, *Easier said than done*, especially if you have been trying not to think about your money. I've had women tell me they would rather walk on hot coals. So, before you start, try these two things.

First, bring your life goals to mind. If you created a visual reminder of your goals in chapter three, place it near your workspace. You are tackling this to put those goals in reach.

Next—and this is important—take a minute to notice how you habitually talk to yourself about your money habits. Many of us have inner voices that say harsher things to us than we would ever tolerate hearing from someone else. If that is happening with you around money—if you tell yourself that you are stupid, irresponsible, hopeless, or anything similar—pay attention. That self-talk is just making you feel incompetent and anxious. It may also be part of the reason why you avoid looking at your finances—which, as we just discussed, can mess you up. You will feel better and perform better on the steps in this chapter and beyond if you inject self-compassion.

Here is an exercise to help you do that. It was created by Kristin Neff, an associate professor at the University of Texas at Austin and a leading authority on self-compassion. The practice I am sharing here, paraphrasing her words, is about noticing your self-talk. It works like this:

1. Think about when a close friend or a loved one is struggling and comes to you for support. How do you respond? What might you say, and in what tone?
2. Think about times when you feel bad about yourself or are struggling. How do you talk to yourself? Note your tone.
3. How, if at all, are these different? What leads you to treat yourself differently from the way you treat others?
4. What do you think would happen if you talked to yourself the way you typically talk to a close friend or a loved one when you are suffering?

Once you are talking to yourself in a way that is supportive, you may be able to reframe how you track your spending. Hopefully, you will be better able to think of this task as financial detective work. You are simply gathering information that you can use to make more thoughtful choices about your money. You will be able to let go of your fear of finding out that you really are incurably bad with money after all. Remember: *No one* is incurably bad with money. We all are capable of change.

You can also think about this financial research as follows: if you don't like what you see now, it will be easier to notice the positive impact of any small change you make!

WHAT WE CAN DO

There are two parts of our financial lives we need to look at to get the full picture: where we stand right now, and what is happening month-to-month. How we use our money month-to-month affects where we stand financially, and where we stand affects the amount of money we have to spend month-to-month. That is why it is important to look at both.

If we're going to use formal names for what we are doing—and why not?—the snapshot of today is known as a personal balance sheet or a statement of net worth. The look at what is happening month-to-month is a personal income statement or a statement of income and expenses.

Step One: Create your personal balance sheet

This statement has three sections: assets, liabilities, and net worth. Here is how to create yours.

You can use paper, an Excel spreadsheet, a digital platform, or the worksheet in the appendix. Whatever feels comfortable is fine.

Assets Come First

These include all your financial accounts: your checking and savings account, an investment account if you have one, and a retirement savings account like an IRA or a 401(k) if you have those. Pro tip: If your employer matches your 401(k) contributions, you may have to stay in your job for a period of years for those contributions to vest or become wholly yours. For your balance sheet, just count the vested part of your employer's match, plus anything you have contributed.

If you own your home, you can include that as well. Use Zillow or another online source to get a current market value. (We'll put your mortgage somewhere else, so just include the market value here.)

Technically, everything you own is an asset, but we are going to stick to financial accounts and assets that you can easily value and would plausibly sell. The clock that your late grandmother gave you is an asset, but putting a price tag on it would be tricky—and chances are you don't want to part with it anyway.

When you have all your items listed, add them up. That tells you your total assets.

Liabilities Are Next

Liabilities are all the things you owe. These include your mortgage if you have one, any money you may have borrowed on a home equity line of credit, and car loans. Student loans are liabilities too. List the full amount you owe on all your loans.

List any money you owe on your credit cards as well, even if you plan to pay it next week. For extra credit, when you list your liabilities, you can also list the interest rate you pay for that debt. Notice which debt has the highest interest rate.

When you are finished, add up everything in this category to find your total liabilities.

Your Net Worth

This is the simplest part mathematically. Subtract your total liabilities from your total assets, and you have your net worth. This is why this is called a balance sheet: your assets—the things you own—should be in balance with, or equal to, the sum of what you owe and your net worth.

At this point, you probably have . . . feelings about what you just learned. Perhaps you just learned that you have a negative net worth. Remember: This. Is. Just. A. Number. All it shows is where you stand today. And your net worth can be small—or even negative—for any number of reasons.

- You may have borrowed a lot of money for education—yours or a child's.
- You may have taken out a big mortgage to buy your home.
- You may be using a home equity line to make improvements to your home.

If you have done any of these things, you have invested in your future. Investments can take time to pay off. On the other hand, if credit card debt is overwhelming you, that is another matter, and in chapter six I will explain strategies to get high-cost debt under control.

In the chapters that follow I am going to show you how to grow your net worth from this point forward.

Step Two: Create your income statement

This is where you take a good look at the money you have coming in and where that money is going. The process of gathering this information may seem tedious, and if you are already pressed for time, it can even be annoying. But I promise that if you make a habit of tracking your spending, it will help you feel in charge financially and you may even find motivation to make healthy changes in your spending.

Plan to track your income and spending for a month for this exercise. A month is the unit of time most people use for budgeting, and it jibes with the frequency of when we pay most of our bills.

1. List your monthly income. This can include your salary from your main job, income from any side gigs, and any other money you have coming in on a regular basis. If your income

is irregular, calculate how much your average income is for a month.

2. Tally up your expenses. Here, you have choices. If you rarely or never use cash, you may be able to complete this task in a day by looking back at all the electronic and paper records of your spending over the past month. But if you do use a lot of cash, you will need to start tracking today and keep it up for a month.

3. However you decide to tally your spending, think next about how you will record what you find. Some people like to carry around a little notebook. Others save receipts and then tally them every other day or so. Still others sign up for online budgeting platforms. You can also use the "Actual" section of the income and expenses worksheet in the appendix. (We will use the "Projected" section later.) There is no one ideal system. The best one for you is the one you will stick with.

4. When you begin tracking what you spend, start with a week at a time. Just tally up all that you spend, and then at the end of the week, sort it into categories: rent, groceries, entertainment, whatever. If you are looking back at your records, you can follow a similar approach. It is a good idea to also notice whether your spending was planned out ahead of time or more spontaneous.

5. Total up each category and then subtract your total overall spending from your income.

Step Three: Review your data

This is your moment to reflect on what you see—*without judgment*. Some of your spending will be for necessities like rent, mortgage payments, or utilities. But some of it will go toward more optional things like hobbies and travel. What do you think about what you are doing? Are you spending your money mainly on things that are truly important to you, or is it going to products and activities that don't matter as much?

What, if anything, are you able to put toward saving given your current spending? How much money could you save for long-term goals if you changed your spending habits?

To be clear, there are times we need to make spending and saving decisions when we are in crisis, and these choices may not reflect our long-term goals. Some of us took short-term financial steps during 2020 just to get through the worst of the coronavirus pandemic, reducing or halting contributions to retirement savings or college funds—or even withdrawing money from those accounts. Many others stopped saving, period, or depleted their emergency funds.

If you took steps like these, please be gentle with yourself. Women lost millions of jobs in 2020 or had to cut back on work to juggle unique circumstances. We were all doing the best we could.

Some of us, in contrast, may learn that we have been spending in ways that keep our long-term goals chronically out of reach because our habits have not reflected our financial realities. Please, try to stay neutral whatever you see. Right now, we are in the no-judgment zone. Wherever you are financially is just ... where you are. If you made mistakes in the past, now you know—and you can learn what to change. This is your moment to start thinking about how to get to a better place, whatever that means to you. You will be happier in the long run if you set intentions to spend and save your money in a way that makes your life goals possible.

Think back to the heartfelt goals you identified in chapter four. Not everything has to be about those goals, but do reflect—again, without judgment—on how your spending can help you progress toward those ideal outcomes.

When I went through this process myself, I noticed that my grocery bill was much bigger than I thought. I realized that I had been busy with work and running into the expensive grocery store near my office a few times a week to grab this or that, and those trips were adding up. Shockingly, buying groceries was not at the top of my list of life goals! I started planning meals ahead and shopping at the large, less expensive grocery store once a week, freeing up cash that I could save or put toward bigger goals.

Similarly, a former client of mine realized she was spending a lot on home accessories she did not need, and she redirected the money toward a summer activity for her family.

REFLECTIONS

I can't tell you how to spend your money so that it is fulfilling for you. That is entirely personal. But numerous studies have found that experiences like the summer activity above give greater and more long-lasting happiness than possessions. New things tend to make us extra happy at first. But very quickly, they just become part of our normal lives. Experiences, on the other hand, can be anticipated, savored, and recalled. When you think about how you may want to change your spending, consider the following from the late Roger Corless, a religion scholar.

"Trying to be happy by accumulating possessions is like trying to satisfy hunger by taping sandwiches all over your body," he wrote in his book *The Vision of Buddhism: The Space under the Tree.*

The key to making your process of reflection effective is to stay mindful about how you are talking to yourself. Try not to scold yourself. Rather, focus on changes you want to make going forward and remind yourself what you will gain.

Patricia made her own healthy changes with a similar process.

Patricia's Story, Part Two

When Patricia came to me, her stress levels were very high. Her husband was still mending, and her situation felt full of uncertainty. Then she realized that she could sequence her financial needs and tackle them one at a time. As a strategic thinker, this process felt familiar to her. She started tracking her spending and looking ahead to identify changes she could make.

As Patricia started to get a better handle on the state of her finances, she began to feel more in control. She saw ways to ease her family's immediate financial strain, and that freed up mental space so she could think about how she might make her work more satisfying—and how she might rise in the organization.

Coincidentally, a recruiter called Patricia as she was going through this process, and she landed a new job that came with a big raise. Patricia's work on her money life did not cause the recruiter to call—but thinking about her finances had helped her think in terms of change and possibility.

WHERE WE GO NEXT

The process of taking a good look at your finances can be challenging on many levels. Just for starters, there can be an awful lot of paperwork involved in getting a full picture of the state of your money. Congratulations on tackling the job!

This can also be challenging on an emotional level, especially if you are unhappy with where things stand for you now. But if you can, think of this task of tracking your spending like a mortgage or a student loan; this work is an investment in yourself and your own future well-being. You are worth it.

Please, pause for a moment to look back at the bottom of the staircase and note how far you have come. You have crafted an empowering money story for yourself, used it to strengthen your closest relationships, and now you have tackled the first piece of your plan for the future.

What if you could set up a system that allowed you to express how you want to use your money going forward, not just for groceries and car maintenance but also for your longer-term life goals?

What if there were a way for you to have peace of mind about your finances, knowing that your money is all set up and in place to cover everything you need it to do? There is, and that is what chapter six is all about.

Chapter Six

Create a Statement of Intent

"Money does stress me out sometimes. I feel an obligation to save, earn, and have a good job. Still, sometimes I am not able to sleep, or am anxious. And I get depressed, honestly. You start looking at your life and thinking what do I work for after all? I hate the feeling of being deprived and feeling like I can't go to that restaurant because I have to be saving."

—Gloria, 40s, manager

"When I feel like there are things I haven't taken care of—credit card debt, for example—that feels like a grip on my life that's keeping me from something. When you have debt or are not making as much as you'd like, it can make you captive to your own life."

—Selena, 30s, social worker

> "*I feel like my entire marriage we've been just hanging on by a thread because of the way we've done things financially. That puts me on edge. I would like to not have that feeling. I definitely do not have three months of expenses covered. I don't have a down payment for a house. I also have student debt. Am I supposed to save or pay down my debt?*"
>
> —Jessica, 30s, social worker

THE PROMISE

When we know where we stand financially and what has been happening with our money, we can step back from in-the-moment issues to consider how we can use our money going forward to achieve our goals. The vehicle to do this is a budget, or (my preferred name for it) a statement of intent. In this chapter, you will learn how to create one for yourself, thereby mapping out a path to financial well-being.

Please meet Rachel, who went through this process.

Rachel's Story, Part One

Rachel, a physician, divorced several years ago. Her children were grown up and living elsewhere, and she took great joy in providing financial support to them in the form of happy surprises—unexpectedly offering to spring for a car repair or vacation, as opposed to regularized support for rent or tuition. She was also saving for her own retirement and future security, but when she came to me, she said that a few times a year she would have to dip into what she had put away to cover her bills.

Rachel was feeling anxious about her finances because she could not understand why she needed to take money out of her savings every now and then. She had a capable financial advisor she liked, and she was saving for retirement, but her financial stress was intensifying. Even so, she had no interest in creating a budget for herself. She said she was afraid of what she might learn and did not want to have to deny herself anything.

WHERE WE STAND NOW:
WE ARE BUDGET AVERSE

The word "budget" brings up all kinds of associations, like self-deprivation and cheapness. Not surprisingly, even though financial experts regularly extol the value of budgeting, a 2021 survey for the financial services firm Charles Schwab found that only a third of Americans have a written financial plan. Two in five have never had a budget, according to the Certified Financial Planning Board of Standards.

> *"I don't like not being able to do things because of my financial situation, so I do them and pay the consequences later on. Like travel, or everyday spending. I spend way beyond my means."*
>
> —Sunita, 30s, manager

Our aversion has several roots. First and foremost, if we are living paycheck to paycheck, a budget can underscore how limited our resources are. I think we can all agree that no one wants to be reminded of a situation like that.

> *"I just try to do everything I can, but no matter what, at the end of the month it seems like I did nothing. I live in a very expensive town. My husband thinks we are living okay, but we are not living okay."*
>
> —Ruth, 50s, teacher

I'll pause briefly here to remind you that many more women than men live paycheck to paycheck, often due to structural issues that are not our fault. If you find yourself with nothing left over at the end of a pay period, do your best not to blame yourself. Rather, use the tools in this book to help you plan your way to greater financial security.

THE MYTH OF OVERSPENDING

Then there is the matter of the implicit messaging we receive every day about women being chronic overspenders. Google the world "overspending" and look at the images that come up. There is a distinct female tilt to them. The same thing happens with shopping.

Think about the magazine and online articles you see about budgeting as well. How many of them have headlines like "How to Budget Without Feeling Deprived"? or "How to (fill in the blank) Without Blowing Your Budget"?

Starling Bank, a woman-led bank in Britain, commissioned a linguistic study of the language used in money-focused articles in women's magazines. The study found that 65 percent of the articles describe women as excessive spenders, and almost 90 percent discuss small ways to save money.

In contrast, in magazines aimed at men, 73 percent of the articles related to money talk about making big investments—in the market, in real estate, and so on. Overwhelmingly, the messages women receive about money habits suggest that we are the irresponsible ones.

It's not true, by the way. Women and men just spend on different things. Bureau of Labor Statistics figures show that for the twelve months ending in June 2020, single women spent roughly $3,200 less than single men spent. Yes, women spent more on personal care and apparel. But men spent more on transportation and entertainment.

> "*I manage money on behalf of my clients, and successfully. But when it's my own money, I get a little lax about my systems.*"
> —April, 30s, event planner

Still, that whole overspending trope can make budgeting feel emotionally risky, if we think all we will find is evidence that we are, as the saying goes, "bad with money."

WHY FAILING TO BUDGET HURTS US

Not surprisingly, it can feel simplest to just let the task of creating a budget slip down our to-do list. But when we don't budget, it can cause problems. Think about what you noticed when you created your personal income statement.

- We may spend more than we intend on impulse purchases. Think about the last time you went to a big-box store like Costco without a shopping list. How full was your shopping cart when you emerged? Right. Without plans, we can easily go off track.

- We may carry high-cost debt for months on end. Just over half of all active credit card accounts were carrying a balance in mid-2021, and the national average credit card debt for consumers with unpaid balances was over $6,500, according to LendingTree.com. With average card interest rates at that time close to 15 percent, if a consumer left that average balance untouched for a year, it would cost them nearly $1,000.

- Without a plan, it is harder to build an emergency fund—a linchpin of financial wellness. Some 51 percent of Americans lack enough savings to cover three months of living expenses, and one in four have no emergency savings, according to Bankrate.

- Our lack of financial cushion was reflected in the fact that many of us tapped our retirement savings during 2020: nearly a third of Americans withdrew money outright from retirement accounts or borrowed from them, and that money was mostly spent on living expenses, according to research by Personal Capital.

- We may save less than we need to for our own future security. In the next two chapters, you will learn all about growing your savings by investing your money—the number one route to long-term financial security. But before you can grow your savings, you must build them up. Without a budget, that is hard to do consistently.

> "I follow advice—I max out the retirement savings, and I keep money going into a savings account. I don't carry credit card debt and I have money to give others. But I don't go beyond that, and I don't keep good track of stuff."
>
> —Sara, 50s, attorney

HOW A BUDGET CAN HELP US

When we go through the process of creating a budget, we lift ourselves above day-to-day financial thoughts. We gain space to think and plan ahead, instead of looking back and regretting behavior we can't change. That is why I like to think of a budget as a statement of intent.

- You can set intentions to spend in a way that reflects your true values and priorities.
- You can plan to build an emergency cushion, paycheck by paycheck.
- You can create a realistic plan to pay down debt.
- You can save consistently for longer-term goals.
- A budget can help you break the cycle of living paycheck to paycheck if that is part of your reality.

A budget also frees up our mental space. I mentioned the nagging unease we feel when we don't have a financial plan. Well, the reverse is true too. Even better, big pieces of your budget can be automated. When your paycheck gets deposited, you can set up automatic transfers to accounts dedicated to different savings goals. And provided you don't touch those accounts, your savings will grow without you lifting a finger. Automating your savings is like a power tool to build your fortress of financial security.

Budgets bring emotional benefits as well. When we know we have our money working for us in service of our goals, we are putting ourselves in a power position. It is almost as if we are saying to our money, "You go do this, and then do that." We start to feel in charge of our money instead of the other way around.

That's a great feeling. It is also financially beneficial: When we feel powerful, researchers have found that we are more likely to add to our long-term savings. We seem to want to maintain that feeling of power. Think what can happen next. We like feeling powerful, so we save more, so we feel more powerful, a positive cycle.

Similarly, a study by Andrew Baker and Ning Tang of San Diego State University found that people with higher self-esteem in general make better financial decisions. There is an indirect link as well. According to Baker, "People with better self-esteem *perceive* themselves as having better financial knowledge, and the *perception* of having better financial knowledge is associated with better financial decision-making."

The truth is, rather than being a surefire path to self-deprivation, a budget, or a statement of intent, makes you the boss of your money, instead of the other way around. It also allows you to enjoy the certainty that your necessities are covered. It is, believe it or not, freeing. How's that for motivation?

WHAT WE CAN DO

You can find any number of templates that will help you create a budget. If you use the "Projected" section of the income and expenses worksheet in the appendix section of this book, you can easily compare your intentions to your current spending. Look around and experiment to find one that you feel you can stick with. You can also consider a digital budgeting platform.

Step One: Add up your income

This is the same process you went through to create your personal income statement. Most of us receive a paycheck on a weekly, biweekly, or monthly basis as our primary source of income. Right now, you are creating a monthly budget, so consider how many paychecks you include here.

You may have other income sources too. Do you receive maintenance (formerly called alimony) or Social Security? You can include that. If you have regular investment income, that goes here too. If you have a primary job or a side gig that generates irregular income, estimate the lowest monthly amount you can regularly expect and add that.

The sum of all these things should equal all the income you can truly plan on every month.

Pro tip: With fifty-two weeks in a year, there will be a few months when you get an extra check. If your cash flow permits, one way to boost your financial wellness is to budget for four weeks' worth of income, but a full month's worth of expenses. Then when those extra checks come in, you can accelerate your debt reduction or add to your savings.

Step Two: Cover your essentials

Your next move is to plan your intended income allocation so it can support your life going forward. First things first: your essential costs of living. These include rent or mortgage, groceries, utilities, and phone. You cannot significantly change how much you spend on these things without disrupting your life.

Make sure to provide for essential expenses that only come up in certain months. Calculate what those essential expenses cost you per year, divide by twelve, and allocate money to cover those expenses.

Step Three: Allocate to core saving

Remember what I said earlier about emergency savings? You need some. In an ideal world, you would have enough emergency savings to cover three to six months of your living expenses. But in truth, any emergency cushion is better than none. Make it a priority to build your rainy-day fund bit by bit.

The same goes for retirement. If you are not saving in a workplace retirement plan, you need to allocate some of your income to a retirement account you create, typically some type of IRA. In 2021, you were allowed to contribute up to $6,000 per year, or $7,000 if you are age fifty or older. I will explain more about different types of IRAs in chapter seven and the appendix. For now, I will just say that an IRA account lets you save and invest for retirement and you get some tax advantages.

Step Four: Plan your debt paydown

When you tracked your spending, you were able to see what you were spending on your debt. Some loans, like mortgages, do not need to be paid back right away. But if you have credit card debt, or other debt with a high interest rate, paying that off should be a top priority, right after adding to your emergency savings. The sooner you get rid of that debt, the sooner you can significantly reduce your expenses.

If your student debt comes with a very high interest rate, make it a priority to accelerate that paydown too.

How should you prioritize these saving and debt-reduction goals? Your first priority should be to build an emergency cushion. Then, think about where you get the best return. If you are paying, say, 18 percent interest on credit card debt, your biggest payoff may come from paying that debt before tackling other priorities. In a similar vein, if your investment return on your 401(k) is higher than the rate you are paying on your student loans—something that is quite possible if you get an employer match—it may make sense to maximize what you contribute to retirement savings and stick to your student loan repayment schedule.

Step Five: Save for other goals

Most of us have things we want to save for beyond the essentials, like buying a home, helping a child pay for college, or traveling. This is where you allocate some of your income to achieving those goals bit by bit.

Note: There are special accounts called 529 accounts that you can use to save for college. If that is part of your plan, consider opening one. I will discuss saving for college in more detail in chapter eight.

How much should you be saving in total for all your goals? One rule of thumb is that if you save roughly 15 percent of what you earn starting at age 25 and invest it appropriately, you should reach retirement with enough savings to give you the income you need for the rest of your life. Fidelity Investments recommends that by age thirty, you have an amount equal to your annual salary saved for retirement. By forty, the goal is to have three times your salary, and by fifty, six times.

These are big numbers, no question. And if you are over thirty—or over fifty—and just starting this process now, they may make you feel discouraged . . . or worse.

There is another way to think about this, however: More saving is better than less. Any saving is better than none. Do what you can, put your money to work in investments (more on that in the next chapters), and you will be taking care of your future self as best you can.

You will also have at least one other income source in retirement in the form of Social Security. You can learn more about how to claim your benefits strategically in chapter nine and the appendix.

One more thing: Automation is your friend for both saving and debt reduction. When you automate saving and debt payments once, you don't have to go through the decision month after month. Call your bank or go online and set up automatic transfers into your savings account. You may even be able to set up different accounts for different goals and automate transfers there. You will be saving and paying down debt and it will be just part of the landscape.

Step Six: The extras

Any money you have left over after you allocate your income among essentials, core saving, and other saving counts as extra. This is money you can use for entertainment, new clothes—whatever you want. Enjoy!

REFLECTIONS

Whew! That was a lot. Take a minute to let it all sink in. How do you feel? At a minimum, I hope you experience a flash of pride for having gotten this done. It's work! But . . . it's possible that when you got to step six, you had nothing left. All your money had to be allocated to essentials and savings.

That stinks, no question. If that happened to you, consider this: *You are solidifying your base.* Your growing emergency fund means a fender bender will not derail your plans. If life brings a surprise—and you know it will, sooner or later—you will be ready.

Your debt reduction is freeing up cash, in the form of reduced interest payments. Remember when I told you that someone carrying an average amount of credit card debt and leaving it untouched for a year could wind up paying close to $1,000 in interest? If you pay off that debt and get that card to zero, you can avoid that cost. Even better, you will be able to use your credit card to build an impressive credit history—which will get you access to better terms on big loans like a mortgage. That will save you some serious coin.

You are also saving for your future, providing for your security tomorrow.

In short, you are assembling the key ingredients to make an integrated financial plan that will help you achieve your life goals. Look at all you have accomplished so far:

- You have a net worth statement that shows you where you stand as you start your journey to financial wellness.
- You have a pulled-together analysis of your past spending, so you know where your money has been going.
- Now, you have a statement of intent for how you want to use your money going forward.

You can use all this information together to make plans. Look back at where you have allocated your money, both for spending and saving. See if your bigger issue is what's going out the door—or what is coming in.

Are you spending more than you intend on things that don't matter to you? If so, use your budget to plan how you will change that. Set activity intentions ahead of time for cutting that unintentional spending so you can spend on things that matter more. Then, when you are tempted (that's when, not if), remember that you are doing this to stay true to your big-picture plan and your goals.

Alternatively, maybe you are living very simply, but you still don't have enough money for extras. That means you could use more income. Can you create a side hustle? Is it time to start thinking about a new job, or negotiate for a raise or promotion?

Your statement of intent may not match your dream plan—*yet.* But armed with the information it provides, you can plan what you will do to reach the balance you want. That is next-level financial wellness.

Rachel found her own financial wellness this way.

Rachel's Story, Part Two

When we first spoke, Rachel was experiencing financial stress because she could not understand why she needed to take money out of her savings a few times each year. She had always avoided paying much attention to her day-to-day spending, but when she realized a look back at the past year could help her get to the bottom of her cash flow mystery, she went to town and created a comprehensive list of all she had spent.

Lo and behold, Rachel found she was spending much more on her kids than she realized, probably because it tended to be spur-of-the-moment. Here is where bud-geting came into play. She added up all she had spent on them in the past year, divided by twelve, and then started systematically saving that amount every month in a sep-arate account through an automated fund transfer. The result? Before long, she had a pot of money she could use for the gifts she loved to bestow on her children. Instead of suddenly spending an unexpected chunk of her monthly income, which often led her to dip into savings, she used money that was already in her "kid" account to surprise them, and she was able to stick to her regular saving and spending plan.

"I used to be behind the eight ball with cash flow, and now I'm in front of it," she said. "It just feels very nice and organized, and I don't worry. It's odd that the planning can make it feel more in control rather than less."

That, in a nutshell, is the value of budgeting.

WHERE WE GO NEXT

The principles behind budgeting and statements of intent are really what this book is about: making your money serve you instead of the other way around.

Just like your new money story, it may take a bit of time before this kind of planning feels normal and reflexive. You may also find that your cash flow feels tight if you systematize—and increase—how much you are saving. You may now be intending to save more than you were, whether for emergency savings or a vacation, or you may be planning to pay down debt more quickly than you had been.

But just as a new purchase starts to become part of our normal landscape over time, a reduction in free cash at the end of the month will soon feel more reasonable. Even better, if you use automated fund transfers to streamline your saving as much as possible, your baseline financial unease will shrink or disappear. You will know that you are covering all your essentials. You can think about bigger things, like making your hard-earned savings grow.

That starts in the next chapter: you are going to become an educated investor.

Chapter Seven

Finance Your Future

||||||||||||||||||||||||||||||||||||||||||||||||||||||||||||||||||||||||||||||||||||||||||||||||||||||||||||||||||||||||||||||||||||||||

"I just never really understood stocks. I think maybe around age eighteen or nineteen, I just lost confidence that I could do something on my own."

—Karolina, 50s, realtor

"I know very educated women—we all have post-graduate degrees, but not in finance. They never taught us finance. I tried taking one class when I was single, and it was a little overwhelming."

—Gail, 50s, physician

"Probably I come up short as far as investing. I'll be the first to tell you—no clue. I don't read anything about it. I leave it where it is. I'm being brutally honest with you. We have savings but I don't really know if I'm putting them in the right places. You have to have trust if you are using someone, or knowledge to trade for yourself, and I'm not comfortable with that."

—Penny, 50s, executive assistant

THE PROMISE

Investing is the area of personal finance where women tend to feel the least confident, for a variety of reasons. But it is also the surest route to future financial security and ease, now and in the future. In this chapter, you will learn the basics of investing for your long-term future—your retirement, hopefully—in a way that is compatible with the rest of your lifestyle.

BEFORE WE START

This chapter and the next are both designed to help you develop investment strategies that will help you grow your savings so you can achieve your goals. Sounds simple, right?

Unfortunately, navigating the world of investing requires some baseline investing knowledge. That is why I have included a section in the appendix where you can find definitions of investing terms, explanations of core investing principles, and some advice on finding the investing help you need if you decide not to do it all on your own.

If you are new to investing or feel shaky on any of the above, like most women I work with, I suggest reading the appendix before you turn to the next two chapters. You can also start reading and then, if you come across terms and concepts that confuse you, go over the appendix until you feel more solid. If you are confident that you understand the basics of investing, dive right in and refer to the appendix if you need it.

No one is born financially literate, and I want to help you get the most you can out of this book. I firmly believe that all of us can learn this material and use it to help us achieve greater financial well-being. Wherever you are on the continuum of financial education, please know that others are there with you—and you are capable of grasping this content. Frankly, we all deserved to learn this material as children. But if that did not happen for you, this is your opportunity.

Daisy, a financial professional, needed some of this material too.

Daisy's Story, Part One

Daisy, a financial professional in her thirties, was highly knowledgeable about many financial concepts, but investing was another matter. When she came to me, she and her husband had been diligently saving but they were not sure how best to make those savings grow.

As a new homeowner with a growing family, Daisy was also anxious about the costs of home maintenance and the effect that would have on their ability to build savings, for themselves and for their children. She and her husband had started buying individual stocks, but neither of them had a lot of time to devote to investing and their approach was mostly scattershot. Daisy worried that they would never achieve the financial security that she suspected other people she knew enjoyed.

"We work so hard to save, but we never reach a level where we are comfortable," she said. She wanted to lose her financial anxiety and make a real plan to grow wealth.

WHERE WE ARE NOW: IN NEED OF A LONG-TERM INVESTING PLAN

I hope at this point you can stop for a moment and notice what you have accomplished. If you have tried at least some of the practices I have suggested in the previous chapters, you are well on your way to changing your relationship to money.

Please also take a minute to notice how you are feeling about your finances. Is some of your tension coming down? Are you able to envision a more positive financial future for yourself? That's a lot, and you deserve to feel proud. Well done! Now you're ready to learn how to make your money grow to ensure your future financial well-being.

It is very, very hard to save your way to financial security. Think about it: If you save 20 percent of your salary every year—which most people fail to do—and you save your money in the bank, at the end of a forty-year career you will have savings that are roughly equal to a little more than eight years (20 percent) of your income. That's impressive—but unfortunately, it is unlikely to get you all the way through a two- or three-decade retirement. If you retire today at age sixty-five, you have roughly fifty-fifty odds of living to age ninety!

Now, it's true that your cost of living will likely go down when you retire. If you are no longer commuting or suiting up to go to an office, life can be slightly less expensive. Even so, you will still need a place to live and food to eat, and you may even want to do some things you have postponed, like travel. Financial advisors often estimate that your living costs in retirement will be 85 percent of what they are while you are working.

If you want to make sure you do not outlive your money, you need to invest your savings so they can grow. Think of it this way: *You work hard for your money. Now you need to make your money work for you.*

BARRIERS TO ENTRY IN INVESTING

Unfortunately, women often doubt our ability to make smart choices regarding investments, and women of all ages often let their partners make the long-term financial decisions. In my own research, women told me over and over again that they felt less confident as investors than as budgeters and savers.

In addition, even if we are knowledgeable about money management, we may lack a well-articulated plan for investing.

Only one in three women have a formal, written retirement plan, according to a 2020 study by the American College of Financial Services, and only one in six say they feel very comfortable with investment considerations related to retirement planning. There are any number of reasons why investing can feel daunting for women who in the past have not focused on putting their money to work.

Barrier 1: Unfamiliar Territory

As mentioned before, parents tend to talk to their sons about money more often than they talk to their daughters. There is more to that: When parents do talk to their daughters, it is likely to be about budgeting, saving, and keeping track of their money. Boys, on the other hand, hear more about investing, credit scores—the kinds of things that will help them build wealth. Only 33 percent of the women respondents in a study by Fidelity Investments reported feeling confident in their ability to make investment decisions in adulthood.

> "*I can manage paying bills and credit cards and keeping track and not falling behind, but I'm not good at longer-term bigger picture stuff like investing.*"
> —Kayleigh, 30s, attorney

Barrier 2: Off-putting Jargon

The jargon thrown around in the world of investing can be hard to decipher. I suspect a lot of it could be simplified. In fact, I know it could. Consider a mutual fund that has in its title terms like US, mid-cap, equity, and growth. Would you understand what that fund invests in? Could you explain that to your daughter? Perhaps this would work better: describe it as a mutual fund that invests mainly in the stocks of medium-sized American companies that the fund managers believe are likely to have above-average growth.

To be sure, you could probably find a similarly jargon-free definition for any mutual fund if you dug far enough into its background information and disclosures. But if the first thing you come across in your investment research is a confounding fund name, it can be easy for a beginning investor to feel that the world of investing is going to be very hard to penetrate.

Consider a conversation that Maisie, a successful marketing executive, shared with me. "My husband said to me that I should probably sell the small-cap fund in my IRA, and I didn't even know what he was talking about," she said. She chalked it up to her being ill-informed about investing—but really, it was the jargon. When I explained that "small-cap" means companies whose overall dollar value, or market capitalization, in the stock market is relatively small—which meant her husband was probably describing a fund that invests mostly in smaller companies—she responded with exasperation, "Well, why don't they just say that?!?" Why, indeed.

Barrier 3: The Other Language Issue

Jargon is just one way the language of investing can be off-putting. Have you ever noticed that the language around investing is kind of . . . male? Think about it. We talk about "building" a portfolio, "beating" the market, "targeting" returns, and on and on.

Researchers from several European universities studied the texts that the texts that potential investors read, looking for common terms and sorting them into conceptual domains. They found that in multiple languages (including English), the words used in investing communications tend to come from domains like war, physical activity, farming, health, and the five senses. These metaphors make us think of worlds that, on an unconscious level, we associate more with men than women, the researchers found.

Does this seem far-fetched? Here is what the researchers had to say: "People are (linguists excluded, perhaps) unaware of the fact that the metaphorical expression 'building your portfolio' is not neutral—until we realize that 'knitting your portfolio' sounds, well, different," they wrote.

WHAT WE GAIN FROM INVESTING

Clearly, there are reasons a lot of women feel uncomfortable wading into the world of investing. But when we do, we are taking a big step toward providing for our own future. A former client of mine I'll call G used to say, "The G today takes care of the G tomorrow" whenever she put money in an investment account or her children's college funds, and she felt proud when she did these things.

She had it right. When we know we can take care of ourselves today and tomorrow, we can live in a more empowered state.

> "I feel a little nervous about having enough for my future life. At this point I barely have any retirement savings. I have a 401(k) plan available at work but I haven't participated."
>
> —Maya, 30s, engineer

There is something else you should know: You may feel a little at sea in the world of investing, but in truth, women tend to be very successful investors. We research investments more carefully, studies show, and we trade less often. The research helps us formulate well-thought-out investing plans and the less frequent trading means we incur fewer transaction costs.

Speaking of plans, investing does not have to be complicated. You will need to know some basic terms and concepts, but the principles underlying a successful investing plan are not complex. In this chapter and the one that follows, I will show you how to keep it simple and still build financial security for yourself.

THE POWER TOOLS AT OUR DISPOSAL

We can maximize opportunities to grow wealth by harnessing the power of time and starting as soon as possible. Anything in retirement accounts can grow without having taxes taken out until you start taking withdrawals, so the sooner you put money to work, the more you can benefit from a concept called compounding.

Compounding as an investment concept works like this: Say you deposit $1,000, and in year one you earn a 6 percent return. You will have 6 percent more in your account, so the balance will be $1,060, an increase of $60. Then in year two, if you earn 6 percent again, your $1,060 will grow to $1123.60, an increase of $63.60. The added $3.60 is growth on your growth. Before you know it, the growth on your growth will exceed the growth from your regular contributions.

You can think about this using something called the Rule of 72. When you divide 72 by the rate you can earn on your investments, you find out the approximate number of years it will take for your money to double. As an example, if you know you can consistently earn 5 percent on your investments, seventy-two divided by five is 14.4, so your wealth will double in roughly 14 and a half years—even without new contributions. The growth starts slowly, but it accelerates thanks to compounding.

Your second power tool is steadiness. You may think of investing as a day-by-day activity, but you will probably fare better if you set your retirement investing plan to reflect your goals and your tolerance for market ups and downs and then ignore it for a month or two. That can be challenging emotionally if the market makes a big move one way or the other. But remember, you are investing for the long term. If your account loses value tomorrow, it could gain it back in a week or a month, and that will not affect your retirement security—which, after all, is the point.

Certainly, it is a good idea to check every month or two to make sure your asset allocation is still in line with your plan. If stocks have a big upward run, they may come to represent a larger share of your investments than you intend, and vice versa. That is a good time to sell some stocks to get back to the asset mix you want. The same principle applies to your bond investments. (An added plus: you will probably be selling securities when their prices are high, locking in gains.)

WHAT WE CAN DO

If you are new to investing for your retirement, you are in luck. This is an area where the industry has invested heavily in making the process simple. You may have access to a workplace retirement plan, and you also always have the option to save for retirement on your own. Your employer or your retirement plan administrator may provide investing help, as will any retirement account provider you use outside of work. You will have different investing choices with each, so we will look at them in turn.

One side note: When you think about saving for retirement, make sure you have your retirement itself in perspective. On average, parents spend twice as much on their adult children aged eighteen to thirty-four as they save for retirement. Even when we exclude education, parents are spending fifty percent more on their kids. That is backwards. You need to save for your retirement. There is no way to borrow for it. And remember, you give your children the gift of peace of mind when you are financially secure later in life.

Step One: Invest at work

Just over two-thirds of all private-sector American workers—and most public-sector employees—had access to a workplace retirement plan, according to 2021 government data. Most of these are so-called defined contribution plans, where workers contribute money and choose investments.

Some workers, particularly in the public sector, are still eligible for an old-fashioned pension plan in which their employer contributes and invests for them. These are called defined benefit plans because the employer's actions determine the size of the benefit you get in retirement. But defined contribution plans like 401(k)s or 403(b)s, where the amount you contribute helps determine your level of retirement security, are increasingly the norm.

More and more employers are automatically enrolling new employees in their defined contribution plans when they are hired unless the employees opt out. If you are not enrolled in yours, now is a good time to sign up.

Defined contribution plans allow you to contribute money automatically through a payroll deduction. That reduces your taxable income for the year. In fact, you do not pay taxes on the money in your workplace retirement account until you withdraw it, which you are allowed to do without a penalty after age fifty-nine and a half. That is why these plans are sometimes referred to as tax deferred retirement savings plans. Most employers who offer these plans will match some of your contribution. That's free money! At a minimum, if you have access to a plan that will get you an employer match, consider contributing enough to get the maximum matching funds. In truth, though, if you can contribute more, that is usually better. We may have decades of retirement ahead of us, and we are going to need a lot of savings to support that. In 2021, the maximum you were allowed to contribute every year was $19,500, or $26,000 if you were age fifty or older.

As for investing the money in your retirement account, workplace plans generally offer a set menu of funds that you can choose from. The funds will hold different securities and types of securities, and they will have different levels of volatility.

If you do not want to select individual funds, your plan may give you the option to invest in what is called a target-date fund. This is a fund where the investment managers regularly adjust the investment mix so that you have a decreasing amount of your money in stocks as your retirement, or target, date approaches.

You are allowed to take your 401(k) money with you if you change jobs, so base your investing plan on your retirement date. You may be able to transfer the money into your new employer's plan, or you can roll money from your current employer's 401(k) plan to an IRA. Read on to find out how IRAs work.

Step Two: Invest on our own

If you do not have a workplace retirement plan, you should definitely try to contribute to a retirement plan on your own, typically some type of IRA. You can also contribute to an IRA in addition to a workplace account, and that will really accelerate your retirement saving.

Some experts recommend contributing enough in your traditional 401(k) to get the maximum match from your employer, and then contributing whatever else you can to a type of IRA called a Roth (or a Roth 401(k) if your employer offers it).

You know from chapter six that you are allowed to contribute up to $6,000 per year to an IRA ($7,000 if fifty or over), unless you have your own business, in which case the limit is higher. That $6,000 may not sound like enough to support you throughout retirement, but it can certainly help. If you do this every year for twenty-five years and your investments earn an average of 6 percent annually, you would have more than $345,000.

You can open an IRA account at any brokerage house, and the process is quite simple. As for what investments to select, all the big brokers offer model portfolios and can talk you through choosing the one that suits your time horizon, risk tolerance, and goals.

Step Three: Automate, automate, automate

When you design your investment plan, you have a simple way to turbocharge the whole thing: human nature. Our brains are wired for what is called inertia. That means that when we have the choice to act or let a situation continue, we will typically let a situation continue unless it is causing us real discomfort. This aspect of human nature can help you with building up your investment accounts if you make your deposits automatic.

You already know how much easier it is to stick to your statement of intent and build an emergency fund by automating transfers into that account. You can do the same with retirement. If you have a 401(k) or the equivalent at work, your employer takes care of automatically transferring funds for you, and you can set up the same process for your IRA. That is harnessing the power of inertia. Rather than having to actively decide each pay period between your long-term future and something tempting in the short run, you make the choice once to prioritize your long-term security, and then you will be highly likely to let that situation continue.

The you today takes care of the you tomorrow, remember?

Step Four: Invest with an eye on your retirement date

When you are investing retirement savings, the general idea is to think long term and have more of your money in stocks the further you are from retirement—subject to your tolerance for risk and volatility. That way, you have the greatest potential for growth early on, and that growth can compound. Then, as retirement draws closer, you reduce the risk level in your portfolio to better protect you against any downswings in the market.

One popular rule of thumb is to subtract your age from 110 and have that be the percentage of your money in stock funds. For example, if you are 45, you would invest 65 percent of your account in stocks. You can adjust your asset allocation each year, so if you follow this rule, you will reduce your stock exposure as you approach retirement.

Both IRAs and 401(k)s let you invest without worrying about taxes, but you do need to keep an eye on your investing costs, in the form of fees on funds. The more you can stick to index funds and exchange-traded funds (ETFs), the lower the fees you are likely to pay. A 1 percent fee may not sound like much, but when you consider that the stock market returns an average of roughly 10 percent every year, a 1 percent fee eats up one-tenth of your potential average return. Many index funds and ETFs have fees under a tenth of a percent. Fees on target date funds can be higher since the manager is actively adjusting the investment mix. More work for the manager can mean higher fees for you, so check on that before you decide to invest.

REFLECTIONS

You may not know a lot about the world of investing. Even with the definitions and explanations you just read, this world may feel daunting. But truly, this is less complicated than you may believe. You have what it takes to be a capable investor.

You can also find a lot of support if you want help choosing funds. Whoever administers your workplace plan, if you have one, is likely to offer educational materials to explain your options. And if you are investing in an IRA, you can keep it simple by using one of the model portfolios offered by your investing platform.

Remember: You are investing money that will stay put for years. Short-term market fluctuations will not affect you. Even more important, there are lots of resources to help you as you become an educated investor. You have a lot of basic information at the back of this book, as well as suggestions for additional resources. Help and support are available, and you *can* grasp this material.

Daisy learned this herself.

Daisy's Story, Part Two

As Daisy and I worked together, it became clear that while she was extremely organized in many parts of her life, that was less true when it came to investing. She and her husband had not been working with a thought-out plan, and they did not feel they were getting ahead.

As we worked together, Daisy realized that a plan was her first step toward financial well-being. She and her husband were already saving methodically; they just needed to take a similarly methodical approach to their investing. She decided that with her job and growing family, she did not want to spend a lot of time on investing, and that buying and holding funds might serve her better.

Daisy and her husband stopped using the investing platform they had when we met. She decided she might reserve a part of their savings for individual stock picking to the extent that it was something they enjoyed, but funds would be the backbone of their wealth-building.

When we finished our engagement, Daisy was actively learning about funds and long-term investing. She was less anxious, more focused, and more hopeful.

WHERE WE GO NEXT

You now know the basics of investing for retirement, and in the next chapter you will learn strategies to invest in a way that supports the rest of your life goals.

Think how close you are! Once you have learned to track your spending, create a statement of intent, and invest your savings so they can grow to generate wealth now and security later, you can start thinking deeply about your life plan. You will be on your way to integrating all you have learned to support your bedrock, couldn't-live-without goals. You are approaching the top of the staircase.

Chapter Eight

Fund Your Life

||||||||||||||||||||||||||||||||||||||||||||||||||||||||||||||||||||||||||||||||||||||||||||||||||||||||||||||||||||||||||||||||||

"I'd like to make an investment that pays off, but it scares me."

—Clara, 60s, journalist

"I'm not completely illiterate with investing in stocks, but I trust my husband 100 percent with it. But I wouldn't suggest that for younger people going forward. My one regret is probably not understanding it better."

—Alicia, 60s, pharmaceutical sales

"I have always been in charge of money for the house and budgeting. Other than that, as far as how to invest—I know nothing. I feel like I'm following in my mother's footsteps."

—Alison, 40s, homemaker

THE PROMISE

Investing for our long-term financial security is important, no question. So is investing that will put your other life goals within reach, now and in the future. In this chapter, you will learn to create an investing plan that will help you achieve all those other goals and live the life you want.

Deborah learned how to do this herself.

Deborah's Story, Part One

Deborah was a successful educator, married with two adult children. She and her husband were living in balance financially, although their communication around financial matters was not as healthy as she wished it were. Then he lost his job in a downsizing, and the family's income dropped sharply.

Deborah had invested money in the past, but she had had a bad experience with an advisor. She remained interested in stocks but was nervous about trying again. While she had a pension coming her way to provide long-term financial security, right now she and her husband needed to reduce their expenses, replace her husband's lost income, or both. Deborah was torn between her fear of having another bad investing experience and her worry about their financial well-being.

WHERE WE ARE NOW: UNSURE HOW TO PROCEED

When we consider investing for retirement, advice is easy to find, whether at work or from a broker. The recommendations we receive also tend to follow common themes: invest as early as you can, focus on the long term, keep an eye on fees, and use accounts that will minimize your tax bill.

When it comes to investing for other goals, though, recommendations vary, and our uncertainty can mount. Should we venture into volatile assets like cryptocurrencies? Stick to super safe but slow-growing choices? Become active stock pickers?

> *"I know enough about money to keep me safe, but I don't get investing one little bit. Trust is a big thing with me when it comes to money."*
>
> —Lynda, 50s, nurse

BALANCING COMPETING PRIORITIES

Then there is the matter of prioritizing goals. Many of us place a high value on helping to pay for our children's college. But there are no hard and fast rules to guide us if we are also hoping to buy a home someday or provide financial support to our elderly parents. It can be hard to know how much we need to invest to achieve any of these goals, let alone the best way to balance all these objectives.

At the same time, we are busy with the rest of our lives, and many of us are just beginning to learn how we can stop living paycheck to paycheck and create basic financial security for ourselves.

UNCERTAIN ABOUT WHERE TO TURN

It would be one thing if we could trust that there were reliable, easy-to-understand sources of advice out there to guide us in building wealth now. But as of this writing, financial advisors do not have to follow a uniform regulatory standard, so if you are looking for an advisor you may find people with all kinds of credentials, like CFPs (Certified Financial Planners), CFAs (Chartered Financial Analysts), RIAs (Registered Investment Advisors), and more—a whole alphabet soup of qualifications that can be hard to decipher.

Those qualifications also come with different responsibilities as far as putting clients' best interests first.

Many financial advisors also contribute to women feeling unwelcome in the world of investing, albeit inadvertently. The industry is trying hard to recruit more women to its ranks, and many of the biggest investment firms have launched initiatives aimed at making women investors feel more empowered and welcome. Still, most financial advisors today are men, and a study by Merrill Lynch Wealth Management found that both male and female advisors often commit miscues derived from old gender stereotypes.

The study even tracked advisors' eye movements and found that in meetings with heterosexual couples, they spent 60 percent of the time making eye contact with the man.

> *"I have a portfolio I don't understand and a financial advisor that helps me with that. I believe it's meant to be like that. The financial services industry designed it that way so that it keeps people oppressed, so they can get paid to do it."*
>
> —Whitney, 40s, interior designer

SITTING OUT

The upshot, not surprisingly, is that women have been less likely than men to invest in the stock market. In one 2021 survey, 48 percent of American women were investing in stocks, compared to 66 percent of men.

The financial effects of the pandemic appear to be spurring some women to become more interested in investing. Among women with incomes over $50,000 and a workplace retirement savings account, half say their interest in investing increased in 2021, a Fidelity Investments survey found. The shift is most pronounced among younger women.

Even so, only a third of the women Fidelity surveyed expressed confidence in their ability to make investment decisions. Similarly, women in numerous surveys are more likely to say they felt anxious or confused about investing, and men are more apt to express confidence.

> *"I hate how complicated it is and how, even when you think you're doing the right things, you may not be. It's also really hard to get what you consider to be objective good advice."*
>
> —Stacy, 60s, writer

THE PROBLEM WITH PUTTING IT OFF

There are several reasons why putting off investing until later can hurt us. Remember in chapter seven when I explained compounding and the Rule of 72? You can't really think about doubling your money unless you are putting it to work by investing it.

Think back to our earlier example of a $1,000 investment earning 6 percent a year. At the end of ten years, that investment would be worth $1,791, a gain of $791. Pretty nice, right?

But look what would happen if you left the money invested for another decade, for a total of twenty years. At the end of that time, you would have $3,208. In the second ten years, your initial investment would have earned $1,417—almost twice as much as you earned in the first ten years. That is why investing long-term is so powerful.

Think back, too, to the wealth gap. Thanks in part to our smaller paychecks, women have a harder time saving as much as men. Investing sooner rather than later is our best opportunity to offset that shortfall. The sooner you invest, the more you have time on your side.

TAKING CARE OF OURSELVES

There is also the matter of our self-sufficiency. There is a good chance we will outlive our spouses, which means we are likely to be on our own at some point. That in turn means that we will likely need some long-term assistance. Long-term care can be punishingly expensive.

Taking care of ourselves is not just about the money though. On a deeper level, we only have a certain number of turns around the sun, as the saying goes. Think back to chapter four, where you identified your key life goals. If we lack the resources to achieve those goals, we can wind up selling ourselves short and struggling to live life on our terms, plain and simple. Investing now will help you amass the resources you need to put those goals in reach.

ARE YOU AN INVESTMENT GODDESS?

Did you know that the word "money" is derived from the name of a Greek goddess? A temple devoted to Juno Moneta, wife of Jupiter, was later used by the Romans as a mint, and the rest is history. We modern women may not get our names on temples, but we can be investment goddesses—or at the very least, thoughtful investors operating from a plan with our core goals top of mind. In fact, we owe it to ourselves to be just that.

One more thing: I hope you finished chapter seven with the recognition that investing for retirement does not need to be highly complicated or time consuming. When you invest for other goals, you can build on what you have already learned. This investing involves different accounts and different tax considerations, but the core process is the same. You mastered the concepts in chapter seven, and you can master these too.

WHAT WE CAN DO

If you want to invest money to finance your life goals, whether that means buying a house, providing for your parents, or something else, the easiest way to do so is through a taxable investment account.

This is probably what first comes to mind when you think about investing. You open an account at a brokerage, and then you choose funds, individual stocks and bonds, or a mix and put your savings to work. Sounds simple, right?

Not so fast. Yes, you open an account, select investments, and get going. But you will be a lot more successful, and a lot less anxious, if you first develop a framework and a plan. Here are four key steps:

1. Identify your goals and organize them on a timeline.
2. Consider your appetite for risk.
3. Consider taxes when you choose investments.
4. Identify tax-reducing strategies for long-term objectives.

Step One: Create your timeline

When you invest for retirement, you have a basic framework. You know approximately when you plan to step away from full-time work, and you can find many evidence-based estimates of how many years you need your money to cover and how to allocate your investment dollars accordingly

Your other personal goals have timelines as well, but it is up to you to set them. Are you saving for a down payment on a house? That's probably a short-term goal. Are you investing with an eye toward travel in your later years? That's more long-term.

Do your best to organize your goals on a timeline and decide how much money you want to allocate to each one from your current savings. You can think of these as goal buckets. Surprises happen and your plans may change, but you will be better served by defining how much you want in each bucket and when you hope to achieve each goal.

Step Two: Consider your risk tolerance

Once you know how long you can leave your money invested for each goal, you can think about how to invest each bucket. For shorter-term goals, things you want to do in the next three years or less, you are better off taking very little investment risk because you will have less time for your savings to recover from a market decline. Investments like certificates of deposit and money-market funds will earn you only a smidgen of interest, but you will have peace of mind knowing that you are highly unlikely to lose your savings.

Let's say you have medium-term goals, things you want to do in the next three to ten years. You can take a bit more risk because you have somewhat more time to ride out a downturn in the market. Experts recommend that medium-term investors emphasize bond funds and add in moderate exposure to less volatile stocks.

If your goals are longer term, you can invest with an eye toward growth by increasing the amount of stock funds in your portfolio. This will increase the risk that the value of your investments will fluctuate. But historically, stocks have outperformed bonds long-term, so if you can tolerate the ups and downs, you are likely to see your investments grow more.

As an example, I have an investment account I hope to use to finance two goals: bucket-list travel far in the future, and a few home improvements in the next year. The money I plan to use for the home improvements is in a money market fund, while the money for the long-term travel plans is invested mostly in stock index funds and ETFs.

Step Three: Consider tax-smart investments

When you are investing in a regular brokerage account (as opposed to a traditional 401(k) account or an IRA), your account will be subject to taxes every year. The amount of taxes you owe will depend on the types of securities you choose and the frequency of trading in the account, either by you or by the manager of a fund you own. In short, you can't control the fact that you will owe taxes, but you have some control over how much.

Awareness of the tax implications of your investing plan is very important. You may be delighted with your investment returns at the end of the year, but if you then turn around and pay a third of them in taxes, your returns will look a lot less rosy—and you will have less money to put toward your goals.

Some types of investments are taxable at the federal and state level, some just one or the other, and some are not taxable at all. In addition, how quickly you sell an investment can affect the rate at which your gain is taxed.

For example, if you buy a stock whose value increases and you sell it after more than one year, you will pay long-term capital gains taxes on those gains. Typically, your long-term capital gains rate will be lower than your income tax rate, but it won't be zero.

If your stock gains value and you sell less than a year after you bought it, you will have a short-term capital gain. The tax rate will be equal to your income tax rate. You will also pay taxes on dividend payments you receive as an owner of that stock.

You can also owe taxes on short-term and long-term capital gains from funds, even if you do not sell the funds themselves. This is especially true for actively managed funds because the investment managers of these funds buy and sell securities in an attempt to outperform the market. Passive funds like index funds and ETFs typically generate less of a tax bill if you do not sell them because the managers of those funds trade less often. (These fund types are all explained in the appendix.)

Income from municipal bonds, issued by state and local government entities, is generally not taxable at the federal level, but your state taxes will depend on where you live and where the bond was issued. The interest on Treasury securities, issued by the federal government, is exempt from state and local income taxes.

At the end of the day, taxes on brokerage accounts are just a fact of life, and there is no one-size-fits-all strategy to maximizing your after-tax returns. That said, it is important to consider taxes as one factor when you choose your investments.

Step Four: Identify tax-smart options for long-term goals

Choosing investments with an eye to the tax implications is one way to be tax-aware—but it is not the only one. Here are two examples of additional ways to keep your tax bill in check, particularly for long-term goals.

Saving for College

Many parents want to help their children pay for college, if possible. More than half of all college students take out loans to help pay for their education, and with average federal student loan debt per borrower at more than $36,000, the impulse to help our children is understandable.

The challenge for parents comes in the enormity of tuition payments. Average tuition at four-year colleges rose 50 percent, even after adjusting for inflation, between 2000 and 2019. In families with more than one child, the financial challenge is even more overwhelming.

There is an investing option to help families finance college, in the form of so-called 529 accounts. (Many special investing accounts—401(k)s, 403(b)s, 529s—are named for sections of the tax code. It's not the most poetic choice, but so be it.)

The reason to consider a 529 account is for the tax savings. You can deposit money in a 529 account, and when you invest it and your savings grow, you pay nothing in taxes. You do not owe taxes when you withdraw the money either, provided you use it for qualified higher education expenses like tuition. If you start early and let your gains compound, you may be able to cover more college costs than you think.

Nearly every state and the District of Columbia offer 529 plans, and you can invest in most of them even if you are a non-resident. There are a few catches, however. For starters, you will need to do a bit of homework to find the plan that is right for you. Many states offer more than one 529 plan, and some states give their own residents special tax breaks. Fees and investment options can also vary widely among 529 plans, so make sure you check what they are.

There are also limitations on how frequently you can trade in the accounts, and your investment options will be limited to the menu of funds on offer through the 529 plan you choose. (If you invest in a target-date fund like the ones available in many retirement plans, the rebalancing within those funds is not limited.) That said, the tax treatment of these accounts makes them a potentially powerful way to achieve a life goal many parents have.

Investing for Your Legacy

You may also be investing with an eye toward leaving a legacy in the form of charitable donations.

If you want to be tax-smart and strategic in your giving, you have a lot of options. Here are two that are relatively straightforward.

- Consider donating securities that have gained value. The charity will receive the full current value of the securities and you will not owe taxes on the appreciation under current IRS rules. You can also deduct the current value of the securities from your taxable income if you itemize your deductions on your tax return.
- Consider making plans to donate part of your future distributions from your 401(k) fund or your IRA. When you start taking money out of those accounts later in life, it gets taxed as ordinary income. But if you direct money from your account to a charity, that amount does not count as income for you.

REFLECTIONS

Whew! We have covered a lot of ground on investing. If you have found yourself puzzled by terms or concepts, please go back to the appendix. You will almost certainly find an explanation there. Please also use this information as a springboard for your investing education. Trust me: if you understand risk tolerance, time horizon, diversification, and the various types of investments, you have enough of a basic framework to become a successful investor. But you can always learn more. Go ahead and explore the Resources page of my website or do your own research. Your goals are worth the effort.

Deborah found that creating an investment plan was both calming and empowering.

Deborah's Story, Part Two

As Deborah and I worked together, it became clear that she enjoyed following the stock market and knew a lot about investing. It also became clear that her long-time financial situation was solid, thanks to the generous retirement benefits she stood to receive. Deborah was facing a financial challenge, no question. But it would only last until she started drawing on her retirement savings or her husband found a new job, whichever came first.

Partly because that awareness reduced her tension, Deborah was able to have a constructive money conversation with her husband. They made a financial plan together and Deborah resolved to trust her own investing knowledge and instincts, stepping back into stock investing with a small amount of cash.

Deborah also realized that with her tension down, she could think about and plan ways to generate more income.

WHERE WE GO NEXT

Congratulations! You have pulled together quite an impressive financial toolkit. You have looked at where you stand financially today and where your money has been going. You have set intentions for how you want to spend and save your money going forward. And now you have learned the basics of investing—for retirement, for your children's college, and, in fact, for anything you want to do.

In the next chapter, you will learn how to use your new-found financial knowledge and clarity in the world around you. We will pull together all that you have learned and built as you have climbed this financial-empowerment staircase. You will see how to make life choices that will affect your financial plan so that it is working to support your life and your goals.

Chapter Nine

Knit Together Your Plan

||||||||||||||||||||||||||||||||||||||||||||||||||||||||||||||||||||||||||||||||||||||||||||||||||||||||||||||||||||||||||||||||||||||||

"Money is the determining factor of my security. When I say security, I don't just mean 'Am I going to be able to eat?' It also gives me a seat at the table. I like feeling like I belong. I have a right to be there."

—Maura, 40s, marketing strategist

"My mom was very frugal, but she always told me you better get a job that pays so you don't have to rely on your husband. That's going to get you through life. Now I have more money than I need, and I like to use it to bless other people. I feel pretty good."

—Jane, 50, nonprofit executive

"Money doesn't represent my worth. It does represent opportunity. I like having enough money to give to things I care about."

—Carolyn, 50s, business owner

"Money for me would represent access. It makes more things accessible to you. It gives you the ability to do things for other people. It does NOT represent happiness. You have to find that yourself."

—Felicia, 40s, political activist

THE PROMISE

You are now equipped with a financial plan where all the pieces connect and support each other. You learned where your money was going, which enabled you to create a statement of intent for spending and saving. The savings you can generate as a result will enable you to invest according to your investment plan to achieve the goals you have articulated.

Your final step in crafting your financial wellness roadmap is to learn how to fine-tune and adjust your plan so you can best respond to the surprises life throws at us all and still support your core goals. In this chapter, you will learn how to use the financial tools and knowledge you have acquired to make decisions that will help you live life on your own terms and achieve well-being.

My former client Bridget faced a challenge just like this.

Bridget's Story, Part One

Bridget was an entrepreneur with two adult children and a husband who also had his own business. Not long before coming to me, she and her husband had sold their longtime home, netting a tidy profit, and had rented an apartment. The sale proceeds were in the bank while they sorted out their next move.

On the surface, Bridget's life seemed good. But privately, she panicked off and on about their finances.

Both she and her husband had incomes that could vary widely month to month. In addition, the sale of their house meant they had no more financial windfalls ahead of them. What they had was what they had, and Bridget worried that it was not enough.

She was anxious and uncertain, and she knew she wanted to find a way to stabilize their finances and plan where they would live next.

WHERE WE ARE NOW

Oh look! I see you, about to reach the top of that staircase. You are up there with a whole lot of newfound knowledge and tools. You have worked on setting big life goals and then creating money intentions to help you achieve them.

You have learned how to "set it and forget it" to build savings and pay down debt. You have learned how to invest your money to provide for your long-term financial security, at work and on your own. You have learned how to invest for other life goals, from financing your children's college, to paying off your parent's mortgage, to bucket-list travel. Underlying all of this, you have crafted an empowering money story full of future potential to carry you into tomorrow.

Time to check in with yourself. Are you feeling proud? Empowered? A little nervous about achieving your life goals right now, even with your plan? Maybe you are feeling all three. So, let's talk about what's next.

ZIGS AND ZAGS

All the work you have done up to now has positioned you so you can progress toward the big life goals you identified. Some of the practices you have in place consist of small steps on repeat, like your automated transfers of money from each of your paychecks to build your financial security. Others involve continuing your investor education and bringing your empowered, confident self to your relationships.

You also understand how to craft an investing plan that will make your savings grow, harnessing the power of time. Now you need to learn how to make sure you can adjust any element of your financial plan so it continues to work for you and support you. Hiccups are going to happen. The only thing predictable about life is its unpredictability, so it's better to know in advance how you might best respond.

Imagine that you are sailing a little boat in the middle of a lake. Somewhere far away on the shore, you can see your big life goal. You know where you want to go, but it is next to impossible to steer straight toward your destination. The winds can shift, the waves may knock you off course, or another boat may get in your way. It is highly likely that you will have to zig and zag to reach your goal.

Money is like that too. And you have a better chance of achieving the future you want if you know how to use a combination of small financial moves on repeat, like automated savings, and bigger life choices about things like retirement, saving, and spending.

> "We are constantly making choices to set ourselves up for success—saving early for retirement, being one of the first to downsize, going easy on vacations, and so on. My biggest fear is to be feeling like I can't do things—I don't have choices."
>
> —Mila, 50s, interior designer

At this point in the book, you are prepared for this kind of planning. We worked on goal setting earlier, in chapter four. Now, with those goals clear in your mind, you also have the knowledge, skills, and clarity to decide if a certain lifestyle change right now to achieve a long-term goal will give you greater *overall* well-being.

SUPPORTING A LIFE CHANGE

Let's say one of your long-term goals is to step back earlier than most people from your full-time, all-consuming career. The Covid pandemic has led many people to rethink their work lives, downshifting or pivoting to pursue work they truly love. (A potentially fatal disease in the air can make anyone rethink their priorities.)

You can adjust your money plan to support a change like that. The big question is how.

Option A is the Big Move. In this case, if you radically reduce your spending by, say, $2,000 per month, you can turbocharge your savings and investing, rapidly building your nest egg to support your new life. But a major spending cut is not for everyone.

A former client of mine, trying to sharply reduce their spending, abruptly decided to sell their home and move to a small condominium. They did cut their spending—but their spouse was miserable, and the relationship suffered.

If you are contemplating a dramatic, immediate change like my former client's abrupt move to a condo, consider: How will that feel in the moment? Will making this change put me or a loved one in an unhappy situation right now? Is that worth it to me, or not?

There are no right or wrong answers to these questions. But considering them before you act will help you think through the ways your Big Move could unfold.

Option B is Slow and Deliberate. Provided you are not in financial peril, you can decide to progress deliberately toward your goal of early retirement by following your budget and slowly and steadily adding to your savings and investments. You may not change your work life as quickly as the Big Mover, but you probably will enjoy your current life more.

Many empty nesters do exactly this, opting to stay in their long-time home even when they no longer need the space, even if it means they will need to defer retirement or give up other things.

This is your life, and you get to choose your path. The key is to have true clarity about the choices you can make in pursuit of your goals. The point of all the financial skills and knowledge you have been building is to give you the tools and the understanding to help you choose your path with clarity and confidence. When you understand how the choices you make can help you—and how they will challenge you, both financially and emotionally—you can make the best decisions for you.

> *"I didn't grow up thinking money was very important. Not to feeling successful. Education has always been attached to my definition of success. Really I just use money to live."*
>
> —Yvette, 30s, social worker

HOW BIG DECISIONS CAN HELP US

Making big life decisions can feel like a lot of mental work. In truth, they often can be. But considering these kinds of choices can turn out to be affirming and confidence-building.

If we carefully consider whether to look for a new, higher paying job, weighing the pros and cons makes us feel in charge of our future.

When you consider these big lifestyle changes in relation to your life goals, the choices you make along with the more immediate changes you are making, like saving on autopilot and investing with intention, will give you a roadmap. You will have a comprehensive plan for using your money in ways big and small to achieve your goals on the timeline you want.

WHAT WE CAN DO

There are many big changes you can make that will have a major impact on your future finances to support your goals. Here are several you can consider, organized by when in your life they are likely to be most effective. You can note action steps you want to explore on the worksheet in the appendix.

Step One: Moves for midlife and earlier

If you still have a decent number of years before you would even consider retiring, some directional investment changes now can make a big difference in your future financial well-being.

- Investing more of your savings in stocks has the potential to increase your wealth, provided you are comfortable shifting to a higher-risk investment mix. If you have a couple of decades left in your career, investing for more growth now can net you more growth compounding later.
- Another money move that pays off more and more over time is increasing your income. In fact, if you successfully negotiate for more pay, whether in your current job or a new one, you can almost automatically boost what you stand to earn in the future. Most employers calculate annual raises as a percentage of what you earned in the year before. You can also increase your income by adding on a second

job or side gig. However you increase your earnings, try to keep your lifestyle unchanged (or mostly unchanged). That way, you will have more money to save and invest, and you can get that growth-on-growth principle working for you.

Step Two: Moves for later-career years

If you feel like retirement is not far off, you may want to try other financial moves. It's a sad fact that older women face age discrimination in the workplace, so angling for a raise or promotion may not work as well. In addition, if you are nearing the financial inflection point where you stop adding to your retirement savings and start drawing them down, increasing your investment risk could leave you exposed to a big market downturn at a time when you can't wait for stock prices to recover. You do have options, however.

- One of the most effective ways to boost your income in retirement is putting off the date when you stop working. I know, this may be the moment where you spit out your coffee. But hear me out. I am not saying you never get to leave your current job. The idea is just to continue generating income from some kind of work.

- More and more people—more than two-thirds of current workers in a recent survey—say they want to work past age sixty-five, even if they change jobs or cut back to part time employment. The financial benefit is obvious, and working later in life can have wellness benefits too. Multiple studies have found that remaining in the workforce in some capacity keeps us engaged in our community and even boosts cognitive functioning.

> *"I have gotten used to the fact that I make good money and I'm very comfortable. But I've determined that once I retire and feel secure, I'm going to go do work with animals, even if it doesn't pay well."*
>
> —Leslie, 60s, nurse manager

- From a financial standpoint, every extra year you are employed is a year when all the retirement savings you worked so hard to accumulate can continue growing. It also means those savings do not have to last quite as long.

- Continuing to work can make another big financial choice possible: It can make it easier for you to wait as long as possible before claiming Social Security. You become eligible for Social Security at age sixty-two. But if you claim benefits then, you will lock yourself into monthly checks that are up to 30 percent smaller than they would be at your full retirement age. Not only that, but your benefit increases every month you wait after your full retirement age to claim, up to age seventy. (You can find more details on claiming Social Security in the appendix.)

Step Three: Money moves for any age

Wherever you are in life, simple changes on a larger scale can have a meaningful effect on your future financial well-being. Spending less and saving more are the power combination to boost your future financial security at any stage of life. Hopefully, you have already created a statement of intent and started these practices.

Big spending cuts can include downsizing your home, giving up an extra car, or turning a planned vacation into a staycation. They can also include reducing the financial support you provide to other family members.

This one cuts deep, I know. But stay with me. Recall my former client Rachel, who was spending more than she realized on her kids. If you are a parent, that impulse may sound familiar. I know I would do just about anything to help my kids, no matter their age. But Rachel found a way to help her children financially while keeping herself financially secure, and you can, too. As noted earlier, many parents spend more on their adult children than they save for retirement. We need to take care of our own financial security first.

Step Four: Weigh the trade-offs

You need to decide whether the short-term tradeoffs of major cuts in spending or resets of retirement dates are worth the potential long-term benefits *for you*. These are big choices—but honestly, you can't get them wrong. As long as you decide whether to cut spending, look for a job, or change your living situation with full awareness of the potential gains and sacrifices that will ensue, you can make the decision that seems best for you overall.

REFLECTIONS

Are you winded? It takes a lot of energy to consider big questions like whether to move, when to retire, and how to support our adult kids. Go ahead, take a breather.

I want you to notice what you are doing in this chapter: You are stitching together a plan for living, informed and supported by all the interlocking pieces of your financial life. You have your big heartfelt goals, which you defined in chapter four. You know where you stood just recently when you created your statement of net worth, and you used that and your spending record to inform your statement of intent for using your money in the months ahead. All those short-term intentions were designed to support you day-to-day as you progress toward your goals.

Then, in chapter seven, you started adding to your investing knowledge and you put together investing plans to build long-term security. In chapter eight, you saw how to use that knowledge and apply it to achieve your other goals with an integrated plan.

Now, you are considering life changes that can further support you as you progress toward your goals.

Will you need to make tradeoffs to achieve your objectives? In all likelihood, yes. Most of us will need to balance short-term and long-term priorities at some point. Some of us may need to refine or redefine our goals. But all of us can benefit from a clear, thought-out, yet flexible integrated plan for using our money to support us.

That is what this whole process is about: using your money as a tool to get you where you want to go in life.

That is exactly what my former client Bridget learned to do.

Bridget's Story, Part Two

As Bridget and I worked together, she realized that she had had several strong-willed men in her life, from her father to her financial advisor, and they had not been shy about telling her what to do with her finances. She also realized that she did not trust herself to make good decisions, financial or otherwise.

As we worked together, Bridget came to realize that while her decision-making process was less linear than that of the men around her, she was perfectly capable of making smart, well-reasoned choices. In fact, she started to see that she made smart decisions all the time related to her business and her family.

Those insights made her more confident that she was entitled to take steps to feel less financial anxiety. And then, she was off to the races. Bridget began talking to her husband about moves they could make to reduce the big up-and-down swings in their monthly income. She started making clear plans to create a new stream of revenue for her business. She also decided she wanted a new financial advisor whose style was more in line with how she liked to plan, and developed a detailed list of qualities she intended to look for when she interviewed candidates.

In one of our final sessions, Bridget wanted to work on a flowchart to make a big home-buying decision. She had stepped into her decision-making abilities, and she was confident about her ability to make large, well-thought-out money choices so she could live life on her terms.

WHERE YOU'VE ARRIVED

Bridget found her confidence. I hope this book has helped you find yours. When you started this book, you may have been anxious about the state of your finances, fearful of what the future might hold, and unsure how to get to a better place. In staircase terms, you were at the bottom, looking up apprehensively at the climb ahead.

Are you feeling greater peace of mind? More confidence? More hope for the future?

You now have a money story that points to your strengths and your potential to achieve better things.

You have a heightened awareness of where you stand financially. You have articulated intentions for how you want to use your money in the coming months, and slowly but steadily, you are building savings to protect you from emergencies and support your long-term financial security.

You have learned basic investing principles and developed plans to invest your hard-earned money to make it work for you and the future you want. In short, you have a full financial toolkit. You are at the top of the staircase, about to step into a more secure, better supported future. I hope you are feeling greater peace of mind, confidence, and hope. You have earned it.

I want to leave you with one last thought. It's from the *Wizard of Oz*. Toward the very end of the movie, Dorothy has a crisis. The wizard has just flown off, leaving Dorothy and her friends seemingly trapped in Oz. Dorothy is desperate to get back to Kansas. Then, Glinda, the good witch, floats in. When Dorothy asks Glinda for help, Glinda tells her she does not need it. "You've always had the power," she tells Dorothy. Glinda then says to the scarecrow and the tin man, "She had to find it out for herself."

With that, Dorothy feels empowered to click her heels and whisper, "There's no place like home." In an instant she is on her way back to Kansas. That is the thought I want you to carry.

You have the power. You also have the knowledge, the money story, and the decision-making skills. You have what you need to put your money to work to help you live life on your terms. I wish you all the best. You deserve it.

Continue the Conversation

|||||||||||||||||||||||||||||||||||||||||||||||||||||||||||||||||||||||||||||||||||||||||||||||||||||||||||||||||||||||||||||||||||||||

"I think my parents didn't want to burden my sister and me with a lot of money talk. As a result, we never sat down and put a budget together or anything. They wanted us to feel freedom and opportunity. In hindsight I wish there had been more discussion and the idea that the freedom comes in knowing what your budget is."

—Lydia, 30s, finance

"Growing up, we didn't talk a lot about money. That was entirely from my upbringing. If you ask to be paid, it means you love money. But now I think if I have a lot of money, I can effect a lot of changes. Like maybe build a school for girls."

—Indra, 30s, engineer

> *"Money was always an underlying issue growing up, and I find myself repeating that to my kids sometimes. I think I'm trying to instill in them a sense of the need to be mindful, but sometimes it comes out as me saying, 'We can't afford that.' I don't want them to feel that it's something we can't control. It's supposed to bring you joy."*
>
> —Roberta, 40s, marketing professional

THE PROMISE

When our financial lives are disorganized and unplanned, it can be next to impossible to think about the world outside our immediate surroundings. But when we have awareness, knowledge, and a financial toolkit, we gain mental space to think how we might better support our community and the people we love. This epilogue is here to help you carry all you have learned into the world around you—supporting the women and girls in your community and your life. If you can take these steps with the girls and women you know, it will benefit you *and* them. It also means you will be taking one small step toward ending women's silence and anxiety around money. You will be bringing more of us into the circle of women supporting each other in this important part of modern life.

Here is the story of a group of young women who embarked on this journey.

THE MONEY TALK, PART ONE

The classroom filled quickly as the high school senior girls filed in for a personal finance workshop. It was near the end of the school year, and their minds were already focused on college and the coming summer. The students settled in their chairs and looked at me politely—but with a distinct lack of enthusiasm.

As I began to ask questions to gauge what they knew about personal finance, a sense of tension started to fill the room. None of the girls wanted to demonstrate in front of their classmates and friends that they did not know something that sounded like it was kind of . . . basic. These girls had just completed some very challenging courses, and they were not interested in challenging questions, at a time when they wanted to feel as if they were on top of the world.

Several girls crossed their arms over their chests. They were prepared to sit through the next hour with me, but it was clear that most of my audience wanted to be somewhere else— anywhere that did not involve talking about money and their financial knowledge.

WHERE WE ARE NOW: PREPARED TO REACH OUT A HAND

Equipped with all your new financial skills and resources, you are in a great position to reach out and lift up the other women and girls in your life so they, too, are financially empowered. If you have children of your own, particularly girls, you can start with them. You can also talk with your friends or even organize a group of women to build your financial knowledge and skills together.

Now, I realize that you may feel taken aback. You may think this whole idea is too much. I can almost hear you muttering, "I just got my arms around this financial stuff! I am not ready to teach someone else."

Here is why this is important. First, we know—often from our own experience—that by and large, parents do not give their children adequate financial education. We also know that girls get less exposure than boys to wealth-building topics like investing.

The Covid pandemic seems to have driven many parents to have more frequent money conversations with their kids, a 2021 T. Rowe Price survey found. But even so, 31 percent of parents still were discussing money with their children once a month or less.

> *"Where I've made mistakes, I think it's because I didn't grow up with anyone to explain it to me. My family doesn't understand finances. So, I was late to sign up for a retirement account at work."*
> —Julia, 30s, social worker

We also know that while most parents believe schools should do more to educate kids about money, as of 2021 fewer than half of all states required personal finance coursework in high school.

College-bound teenagers are asked to make incredibly consequential financial decisions related to paying for their education. Without financial knowledge, they may not understand the implications of the choices they are making if they take out loans, but such choices can have a major impact on their financial well-being as adults. The need for financial education is especially acute among children and teens from low-income families or who are planning to be the first in their families to attend college. Their parents may have less experiential knowledge of their own to share—and decisions around financing higher education can have a big long-term financial impact.

Apart from college, at age eighteen, young people are allowed to apply for credit cards on their own. Without awareness of how to use credit in a healthy way, the potential for major problems is obvious.

You also know that many, many adult women are walking around under a cloud of financial anxiety and uncertainty. So many of the women you heard from in these pages are capable, successful women—like you!—but they are unhappy about their relationship to their money. Often, these women are unsure where to turn for help. You can start that conversation.

OWNING YOUR ABILITIES

You may doubt that you have the chops to take this on, but I believe you do. Even if you don't feel comfortable teaching children or teens about stocks and bonds, you can teach them how to track their spending and set intentions for spending and saving.

- Think back to how you felt when you first started this book. Were you happy with your financial life? What kind of person did you feel like when you had to deal with money tasks? Wouldn't it be nice if the next generation did not have to feel that way?
- If we can spread financial education among American children, there is a chance that it can reduce the yawning economic inequality we face now. If we teach money skills to the next generation, especially the girls and young women, we can create lasting financial empowerment for women.
- If we can help our friends, sisters, and neighbors feel stronger and more capable financially, they will be better able to put their money to work to achieve their goals for themselves and the world around them.

If all this still sounds like too much to take on, consider the science. When we help other people, it makes us happier too.

Sonja Lyubomirsky, a professor of psychology at the University of California, Riverside, and a leading authority on happiness, has identified twelve steps we can take to become happier. Not surprisingly, things like learning to forgive and savoring life's joys are on that list. But so is the practice of random acts of kindness. If you can help someone else feel financially confident from the get-go, that is truly kind. And if Lyubomirsky is right, that someone will feel better and so will you.

WHAT WE CAN DO

There are any number of steps we can take to share our financial knowledge with the women and girls around us. You would be surprised how far a little information can take someone, not just with what they know but with how confident they feel.

Step One: Everyday education, early

To educate our own children about finances, a great approach is to start early and make personal finance a normal topic of conversation as opposed to a taboo subject. When children are very small, we can show them what coins and dollar bills are worth. Over time, they can see what it means to exchange a coin or a dollar for something else.

When they are old enough for an allowance, that can be another teaching tool. Most families link allowances to the execution of chores, which does link the concepts of work and earning money. Be careful about the values you assign to different tasks, though. A recent survey found that boys get paid roughly double what girls do for household chores, thanks in part to boys generally being assigned chores that require more physical labor.

> *"I grew up with an allowance linked to chores. I started working—babysitting—at twelve or thirteen. I always learned that hard work equals money equals what you want. But my parents never talked about finances in front of us."*
>
> —Courtney, 30s, sales

An allowance also gives us the opportunity to talk about concepts like spending, saving, and sharing. In some families, parents have their children allocate a third of their allowance to each of those buckets.

Even certain holidays can provide money lessons. Think about it: When kids trade candy after trick or treating on Halloween, they are expressing the value of different sugary goodies. When they choose the street where they expect to reap the biggest haul, they are learning to invest their trick or treating time to get the highest return. Thanksgiving can offer different lessons about gratitude and sharing with others.

As children grow, they can learn to take responsibility for certain kinds of financial decisions and planning. In middle school, we can give them a fixed amount for back-to-school supplies and make it their job to buy everything they need and stay on budget, for example. Another option is to ask older children to plan parts of vacations, like the best budget-friendly transportation and discounted tickets for tourist attractions.

Step Two: Education about education

As children reach their teenage years, they can start learning the basics of college and money. Parents often tell me that they do not want to worry their children with these issues. I have even heard this from parents of high school sophomores and juniors, who may already be looking at different colleges and starting to dream.

Trust me: Kids know that college is painfully costly for most families. They talk to each other, and they absorb social media messaging. When we don't talk about paying for college and indicate that it is something families can tackle as a team, our children do not have an opening to ask questions and their uncertainty can mount.

If you are striving to pay for your own children's college, please understand that there is no one right way to do this. Do you want to help each child equally? What are their goals? Is one of your children headed for a community college while another wants a private four-year experience followed by graduate school? Remember, too, that you need to balance paying for college against your own future financial security. Both are important.

> *"I don't want to pay every penny for my children, but I am struggling with the balance—making sure they have enough but not so much they don't take responsibility."*
> —Laura, 40s, teacher

There are no right answers here. Everyone's circumstances and values are different, so just make sure that your approach to financing college is aligned with your values and goals. Then, when you know how and how much you plan to provide for your kids' college, you can bring them into the discussion. They will feel more ownership of the financial choices you make as a family in this regard, and they will learn important lessons from watching you grapple with this financial challenge.

Step Three: Teaching credit safety

As children approach their later teen years, they gain access to a powerful financial tool. That tool can help them in life, and it can also trip them up big time. I'm talking about credit cards.

If your eighteen-year-old successfully applies for a credit card without understanding how to use it safely, they can cause themselves significant financial problems.

We discussed in chapter six the fact that credit card interest is punishingly high. If a teen does not realize that credit card bills need to be paid in full to avoid interest charges—and many do not—it can become very expensive for them very fast.

Worse, a teen who overuses a credit card can wind up with a

problematic credit history. That in turn can interfere with their ability to rent an apartment, finance a car, and more.

On the flip side, a credit card can be a useful tool to build a positive credit history, which will give them a high credit score. If you teach a teen to use a credit card every month for a small purchase, and then pay the bill as soon as they see the charge appear in their account (or automatically), they will build a track record of financial responsibility which can net them a good credit score. They will also be learning to spend only when they have money on hand to pay for whatever they are purchasing.

Step Four: Woman to woman

On the opening pages of this book, I asked you to think about how often you talk to other women about the details of your financial life. Most of us just don't. We guard the secret of our salary, and we certainly don't talk about how much money we have in the bank.

The thing is, when we have that conversation, we gain a lot. Right away, we can find out that other people face the same challenges we do. We can also find out information that helps us do better financially.

A former client of mine managed to negotiate a healthy bump in pay after she and her colleagues told each other what they earned. That and some industry research empowered her to land a new job with a major raise.

REFLECTIONS

Starting money conversations may seem minor and unimportant, but this small act truly will make a difference—and it costs you nothing to be charitable in this way. As you know from the introduction, I made my fair share of financial mistakes in my twenties. I have been determined ever since to keep that from happening to others if I can, and now you too have the knowledge and the skills to launch the women and girls in your lives on their own journey to financial empowerment.

The high school girls in my workshop certainly changed their feelings about money.

THE MONEY TALK, PART TWO

The girls attending my workshop on money management were hesitant to engage. But when I mentioned credit cards, the classroom started buzzing. The girls loved the idea that you can use a card to build a credit history, and that done right, it costs nothing. They also were indignant when they learned about credit card interest rates.

The energy really shifted when they teamed up to create a new spending plan for a fictional woman who wanted to take the job of her dreams but would need to live on a lower salary. They started brainstorming and coming up with creative options. There was whispering, there were exclamations, and there was *a lot* of scribbling. After they finished, I had them share their solutions out loud. Clearly, they were energized by the idea that they could make choices like the ones they identified to help them pursue their own life goals. Then the questions started flying:

- Should I open a new bank account at college?
- Can you talk about taxes?
- How can I learn more about investing?

The rest of the hour flew by. As we closed the session and the girls walked out, they were still buzzing. One whispered to her friend, "I am *so* doing that thing with the credit score."

That is financial empowerment. Let's spread the word. Together.

Investing Jargon, Translated

As a journalist, I used to ask my sources to explain complicated financial events or concepts they were describing in terms my mother could understand. It made them stop and think about how best to clarify their message, it helped my readers understand things that may have been opaque before, and it taught me how to demystify the world of investing for people who needed that information.

My goal is to give you that same clarity. Here we go.

WHAT ARE THE BASIC TYPES OF INVESTMENTS?

When you invest, you mainly invest in **securities** like **stocks** and **bonds**. When you buy a **share** of **stock**, you are becoming a part owner of a company. A big company like Apple will issue billions of shares, so your ownership stake is not going to be big enough to tell the CEO what to do. But the value of your stock will be affected by the actions the CEO takes.

Say the company you invest in decides to start selling its product in a new market. It spends a lot of money to open stores, hire staff, and so on. If the product is a flop and the company loses money on the whole venture, the value of your stock may go down. If your company goes out of business, the value of your stock can go to zero. But if the product is a major hit and the company makes more money as a result, the value of your stock will probably rise—possibly quite a bit.

The price of your stock could vary for other reasons too. News of changes in the economy—or expectations of those changes—can cause investors to buy or sell stocks en masse, and that can move the price of your shares regardless of what is happening at the company that issued them.

Some stocks pay **dividends**. These are regular payments to investors, typically every three months. The **dividend yield** is the annual dividend expressed as a percentage of the price of a stock. If a company's stock price is $90 and the stock pays a 75-cent dividend every three months, or $3.00 every year, the dividend yield would be 3.3 percent.

Typically, companies that have been around longer and are more established are the ones that pay dividends. Newer startups need their cash to invest in growth, so they are less likely to pay it out to investors in the form of dividends. Some investors like dividend-paying stocks because dividends are a relatively stable part of the return they will receive. But companies with dividend-paying stocks are often growing at a slower pace. Newer startups have the potential to be riskier investments but may offer greater potential for **appreciation**, or an increase in value.

A **bond** is essentially a loan to a company (or a government). Every bond has a date when it is due, just like a loan. The company will pay you **interest** on your bond, and then when the bond comes due, they will pay you back the face value of the bond. Your bond will not gain or lose a lot of value if the company sells a product in a new market. You'll keep getting your interest no matter how the product does.

Bond investing is not without its risks, though. If interest rates rise and you decide to sell your bond, you may have to sell it at a discount. It is also possible that the company (or government) that issued the bond will **call** the bond before it is due to mature. You will get back the value of the bond, but you will then need to find a new way to invest your money. There is also the risk that the company or government entity that issued the bond goes bust and defaults, or fails to repay you. But in general, bonds are considered to be a safer investment than stocks.

There are several major types of bonds: **Treasury bonds** (and their short-term cousins, **Treasury bills**), issued by the federal government; **municipal bonds**, issued by states, localities, and some government agencies; and **corporate bonds**, issued by (you guessed it) companies.

Treasury securities are considered extremely safe because they are backed by the federal government. They are subject to federal income taxes, but generally exempt from state and local taxes. Municipal bonds, on the other hand, are not taxed at the federal level, and they are not subject to state taxes in the state where they were issued. Investors receiving corporate bond interest need to pay both federal and state income taxes on it. The riskiness of municipal and corporate bonds depends heavily on who the issuer is.

Typically, stocks tend to gain and lose value much more often, and in much bigger swings, than bonds. Investors call that **volatility**. But over the long haul, if you smooth out the ups and down, stocks as a group have tended to perform better. Over nearly the past century, stocks have returned an average of 10 percent per year, roughly double what government bonds returned—though with more variation.

If you are saving for a short-term goal, you will want to consider investment options that are lower risk than stocks or bonds. These are things like **money market funds** or **certificates of deposit**, also known as **CDs**.

A money market fund is a type of mutual fund that invests in very short-term, very low-risk assets. You will get higher interest than you will in a savings account, and money market funds are generally considered very, very low risk, but money market funds are not federally insured like savings in a bank.

CDs have a set term like six months or a year, and because of that, a bank will pay you higher interest on a CD than on money in a savings account that you could withdraw at any time. You are not going to lose money with a CD, but you do tie up your money for some fixed amount of time.

HOW DO YOU DETERMINE
THE BEST INVESTMENTS FOR YOU?

When you formulate an investing plan, you need to be clear on several concepts. The first is your **risk tolerance**. Investors who are relatively comfortable with the ups and downs of stocks are said to have a higher risk tolerance, and they will tend to put more of their money in stocks. Investors with a lower risk tolerance will be more likely to lose sleep when their investments dip even a tiny bit, and they will be comfortable owning more bonds.

Another factor in formulating your investing plan is your **time horizon.** The longer you can keep your money invested, the more risk you can afford to take. If you invest money you want to use to pay for your newborn baby's college, you can afford to wait out short-term ups and downs in the stock market. On the other hand, if your baby is now a teenager, you may want to take less risk—and shift your investments away from stocks and toward bonds and cash.

Diversification is another consideration. Remember how I gave the example of an individual stock losing some or all its value because of something that happens with the company that issued it? If that happened to the only stock you owned, you would lose all your money. But if you owned two or three or ten stocks and the misfortune befell just one company, the impact on your overall investments would be smaller. That is why it is a good idea to diversify your investments. Your portfolio may not gain value as rapidly as the hottest stock you own, but your losses won't be nearly as large.

HOW WILL YOU ASSESS YOUR PERFORMANCE?

When people talk about how the stock market is doing, they generally refer to the performance of a **market index**. These are baskets of stocks whose performance is considered a benchmark, or measure, for different parts of the market. The **Dow Jones Industrial Average** of thirty stocks used to be the bellwether index, but it consists of very large companies and only a small number of them. Some experts prefer to focus on the performance of the **Standard & Poor's 500**, or **S&P 500**, which as the name suggests, includes the stocks of five hundred large companies. The other major index is the **Nasdaq Composite**, which includes thousands of stocks listed on the Nasdaq stock exchange.

Those are just the basic terms you need to know, but they can take you a long way toward formulating your investing plan.

ARE YOU A STOCK PICKER OR A FUND INVESTOR?

Once you are clear on your tolerance for risk, your time horizon, and the importance of diversification, you can start deciding *how* you want to invest. Many people think investing means learning the mechanics of **stock picking**. You can—but there are downsides.

- The first downside is that you will need to devote a lot of time to do it well. Even if you plan to buy stocks and hold them for a long time, picking those stocks will involve a fair bit of research and analysis.
- The second downside is the risk factor. Remember what I said about diversification protecting you from big swings in an individual stock's value? Unless you plan to commit the time to select a wide range of stocks from companies of all sizes across multiple industries, you may be exposing yourself to more investing risk than you realize. In the early 2000s, technology stocks cratered, and millions of people who had invested heavily in them took major losses.
- The third downside is the state of the market today. In 1982, one hundred million shares traded in one day on the New York Stock Exchange for the first time. Today, billions of shares trade daily. In addition, while individual investors directly owned more than 80 percent of stocks in 1960, today big institutions like pension funds and mutual funds now dominate stock trading, often using computerized trading models that can buy and sell in nanoseconds. It is extremely difficult for individual stock pickers to succeed in that environment.

Happily, there is a simpler, less time-consuming approach you can take to investing in stocks and bonds. This is the approach taken by nearly all individual bond investors and a strong majority of stock investors. I'm talking about investing using **mutual funds and their close cousins, exchange traded funds**. Funds are essentially baskets of securities. Some hold only stocks, some hold only bonds, and some hold a mix. Funds are hands down the easiest way to diversify your investments. You buy a fund just like you buy a stock or bond, but lo and behold, you suddenly own a whole basket of different stocks and/or bonds.

Now, there are different ways for the managers of those funds to manage those baskets, and you will wind up paying them fees for their service. That is why it is important to consider the types of funds you choose.

Actively managed mutual funds are just what the name implies: the managers of those funds actively buy and sell securities based on their own research and judgment to try and outperform the overall market. It's a lot of work, and that shows in the fees on most actively managed funds.

You can find actively managed funds that take many different approaches. Some focus on stocks that the managers believe have exceptional growth potential. Others emphasize securities the managers believe are undervalued. Some managers focus on the momentum in the stock market or try to gauge what products consumers will be buying next, and therefore which industries to invest in.

It would be one thing if actively managed funds did indeed produce higher returns than the market. Many do—for a little while. But at this point in the twenty-first century, with the markets as large and complex as they are, and with so many big players making nearly instantaneous trades, it is next to impossible for even the smartest active fund managers to beat the market over an extended period. In fact, over the ten years ending in June 2021, 83 percent of actively managed US stock funds holding large-company stocks underperformed the S&P 500 index. Even in the twelve months ending in June 2021—the kind of tumultuous time that is supposed to favor actively managed funds—some 58 percent of those actively managed funds underperformed. All of this suggests that the high fees on actively managed funds may not be the best way to spend your money.

Passive funds take a different approach. The managers of these funds do not try to beat the market, or a benchmark measure of the market like the Standard & Poor's index of 500 stocks. They do not actively buy and sell securities based on their research and judgment; rather, they put together a fund that includes stocks and bonds that mirror a given benchmark. That is less work for them, and their fees are lower as a result. For investors, passive funds will not beat the market measure they replicate. But passive funds are designed to come very close to tracking it, minus their typically small fee. Will your savings double in a year? Highly unlikely. But a passive fund that closely tracks a market benchmark may well perform better than an actively managed fund—even before fees.

In general, there are two types of passive funds: **index funds** and **exchange-traded funds (ETFs)**.

Index funds do what their name says: they track some index of stocks, like the Nasdaq 100, a group of the largest, most active stocks on the Nasdaq stock exchange. Most exchange-traded funds are broadly similar. Often, exchange-traded funds have lower fees—but not always. And a small but growing minority of exchange-traded funds are actively managed, so if you are interested in passive funds, be sure you are choosing the type of exchange-traded fund you want.

HOW MUCH HELP DO YOU WANT?

One big question to ask yourself as you go about setting up your investing plan is the level of investing assistance you want. Some people are perfectly happy managing their investments on their own, while others want high-level handholding, and still others want an in-between level of support. They are all available, but you need to know what they will cost and the provider qualifications that will help you find unbiased, quality assistance.

The DIY Approach

If you want to invest on your own and choose your own funds, it is easier than you may think. You will need to open an account with a brokerage firm, ideally one that allows you to choose among a wide array of low-cost funds.

To help you start deciding which type of funds to buy, you can look up the mix of stocks, bonds, and cash—the **asset allocations**—that different firms recommend. For example, Schwab offers three basic asset allocation models, depending on how comfortable investors are with risk. Fidelity offers eight model portfolios. The portfolios with the biggest share of investments in stocks are the ones where you also have the greatest prospects for long-term gain, but where the short-term value is likely to fluctuate most. Again, the longer you can leave your money invested, the more risk you can afford to take, subject to your own risk tolerance.

Using a Digital Investing Platform

If you do not want to choose your own funds, one of the lower-cost types of assistance available is called a **robo-advisor**. As the name suggests, this is an automated digital platform that will help you choose among different portfolio models. You will receive little or no human input with this option, but the costs are quite low as a result.

Working with a Financial Advisor

If you prefer to work with a personal advisor, you have a few options. For example, you can hire someone to perform a specific service. This person could draw up an investment plan for you or help you decide how to save and invest for your child's college. You can then take the plan and implement it yourself.

You can also work with an advisor who helps you long-term. They may even do the investing for you, and they can also keep tabs on how your portfolio is doing and recommend changes to keep your investing in line with your plan.

Obviously, these more hands-on advisors can have a major impact on your financial well-being. So, while it may seem tempting to disengage and have the advisor let you know if a problem crops up, that is *not* a prudent approach. For the sake of your own financial health—and your sense of self-efficacy—it is important to keep tabs on how your investments are performing.

Think of it like housekeeping. I would be the first person to say that a dust bunny here or there never hurt anyone. But if you never clean the place where you live, you'll eventually have problems.

If you choose to hire a financial advisor, be aware that anyone can theoretically call themselves a financial advisor, and not every advisor follows the same standards in terms of putting investors' best interests first. Make sure any advisor you hire does make your best interests their top priority. This is known as following the fiduciary standard.

Certified Financial Planners, or CFPs, follow the fiduciary standard. So do advisors with the CFA, or Chartered Financial Analyst, designation. Advisors who follow the fiduciary standard and whose only compensation comes from client fees are often members of the National Association of Personal Financial Advisors, or NAPFA. Remember this: you are entitled to ask any potential advisor how they are compensated and by whom, and what standard of client care they follow.

The way you pay an advisor can vary as well. Financial advisors who perform one-off services, like designing a college savings plan for you, may be paid an hourly rate for their work, or they may charge a set fee for each service.

Others, including many advisors who manage your investing for you, will be paid a percentage of the assets they manage. Their fee gets withdrawn from your investment account every quarter and can range from less than 1 percent to 2 percent or more. That may not sound like a lot—but remember: Over the past century, stocks on average have returned 10 percent per year, and bonds a lot less. If you are paying someone a tenth of that return or more, you and they need to be clear on what is expected of them in terms of service and communication.

RETIREMENT INVESTING ON YOUR OWN

One easy way to invest for retirement outside of a workplace retirement plan is through an Individual Retirement Account, or IRA. There are several types. In a traditional IRA, your contributions may be tax deductible, depending on your income and on whether you have access to a 401(k) plan or something similar at work.

Either way, when you invest your contributions in a traditional IRA, you do not pay taxes on your gains right away. Rather, when you start withdrawing money after you retire, the money you take out will be taxed like ordinary income.

You also have the option to contribute to a Roth IRA if your income is below a threshold set by the IRS. Unlike a traditional IRA, your Roth IRA contribution is not tax deductible. You pay income taxes on the income you contribute. However, once you do that, you will never owe taxes on those contributions again—or on the gains they generate when you invest the money.

With both a Roth IRA and a traditional IRA, you are only allowed to contribute a maximum of $6,000 in 2021, or $7,000 if you are age fifty or above.

A **traditional IRA** can help you if you have higher income now than you expect in retirement—as many of us do. Your contribution will reduce your taxable income in a year when your tax rate is high, and when you pay income taxes on it in retirement, your rate, in theory at least, will be lower.

A **Roth IRA** is a great option if your income is low now and you expect it to be higher when you retire. Paying income taxes on your contribution when your tax rate is low will cost you less than paying income taxes at a higher rate later in life.

A third type of IRA, called a **SEP IRA,** is for people who own their own businesses. With a SEP IRA, you essentially contribute money to the account as the employer. (You do not contribute as an employee of the business.) Your contribution limit is higher, as of 2021 up to the lesser of $58,000 or 25 percent of the employee's (your) income.

SOCIAL SECURITY AND RETIREMENT

Depending on your years in the workforce and your income, Social Security may be a major source of financial support for you in retirement. You are eligible to claim regular Social Security benefits starting at age sixty-two. But before you rush to claim, take a minute to learn how your payments can change if you wait.

If you look up your projected benefits—which you can, at www.ssa.gov—you will see a chart that shows how your monthly benefit increases if you wait to claim Social Security. It's impressive.

Let's say that your benefit at your full retirement age, probably between sixty-six and sixty-eight, is $1,000 per month. If you take it the minute you are eligible, your monthly checks for the rest of your life will be 25 to 35 percent smaller. On the flip side, if you wait and claim your benefits after your full retirement age, the monthly check you stand to receive will increase 8 percent per year. All told, your monthly benefit can increase more than 70 percent between the moment you are eligible and age seventy.

To be sure, if you wait until you are seventy, it will take a while for your cumulative payments to equal what they would have been if you claimed at age sixty-two. But in your mid-eighties, they will equal out, so if you expect to live longer than that and you can afford to wait, consider claiming later. We all have different medical histories and cash flow needs, so you need to decide what is right for you. Just keep in mind what can happen for you if you wait to claim your benefits.

IF YOU ARE IN A FINANCIAL JAM

If you are in a precarious financial situation, long-term planning may feel out of reach. You may need to take immediate steps to shore up your finances. For help with this process, you have a variety of resources and service organizations, many of them local. Here are some national organizations that can help you achieve a measure of stability so you can make a longer-term plan.

Debtors Anonymous offers a twelve-step program for people who want help with their efforts to stop incurring debt. They have chapters across the country.

The **National Foundation for Credit Counseling** provides counseling, usually over the phone, to help people struggling with debt and seeking greater financial health.

The federal **Consumer Financial Protection Bureau** offers basic financial education, links to other resources, and a venue to file complaints about violations of consumer financial laws.

The federal government also has a website, **Help with Bills**, that provides links to various state and federal emergency financial aid programs.

Appendix

Worksheets

YOUR MONEY STORY

Use this worksheet as you proceed through the exercises in Chapter One. You may find it helpful to revisit your answers as you proceed through the book.

1. How do I feel about money?

_____

_____

_____

_____

_____

_____

_____

_____

_____

_____

2. What does money represent for me?

_____

_____

_____

_____

_____

_____

_____

_____

_____

_____

3. Where do my feelings about money come from?

_____

_____

_____

_____

_____

_____

_____

_____

_____

4. What have I learned to believe about money given the experiences I've had?

_____

_____

_____

_____

_____

_____

_____

_____

_____

YOUR LIFE GOALS

Use this worksheet as you proceed through chapter four. These exercises will help you identify core life goals and a path to achieve them.

1. Imagine that it is five or ten years from now and everything has gone exactly the way you wanted. Ask yourself: Where are you? What does your home look like? How are you spending your time? Who are you with?

    Answer in as much detail as possible.

2. Imagine that you are at your retirement party. What will you regret not having done in your life? In an ideal future, would you still do these things?

_____

_____

_____

_____

_____

_____

_____

_____

_____

_____

_____

_____

_____

3. Imagine a day that you would be happy to have on repeat and describe it in as much detail as possible.

_____

_____

_____

_____

_____

_____

_____

_____

_____

_____

_____

_____

PERSONAL NET WORTH STATEMENT

WORKSHEET

Date Prepared: _____

Name: _____

ASSETS

Liquid Assets

Cash and cash equivalents $ _____
Money owed to you $ _____
Life insurance cash value $ _____

Personal-use Assets and Investments

Residence (if owned) $ _____
Investments $ _____
   a. Personal investment accounts $ _____
   b. Retirement accounts $ _____
   c. Investment real estate $ _____
Business owned $ _____
Other assets $ _____

Total Assets $ _____

LIABILITIES

Short-term

Rent $ _____
Utilities $ _____
Credit card balance $ _____
Taxes $ _____
Other $ _____

Long-term

Mortgage $ _____
Auto loan $ _____
Education loan $ _____
Other loan $ _____

Total Liabilities $ _____

NET WORTH SUMMARY

Assets $ _____
Less liabilities $ _____
Equals Net Worth $ _____

INCOME AND EXPENSES, ACTUAL AND INTENDED

Actual Monthly Income	
Income 1	
Extra income	
Total monthly income	

Projected Monthly Income	
Income 1	
Extra income	
Total monthly income	

Housing			
	Actual Cost	**Projected Cost**	**Difference**
Mortgage or rent			
Phone			
Utilities			
Water and sewer			
Cable			
Maintenance or repairs			
Other			
Subtotal			

Insurance		
	Actual Cost	**Projected Cost**	**Difference**
Home			
Health			
Life			
Other			
Subtotal			

Children		
	Actual Cost	**Projected Cost**	**Difference**
Medical			
Extracurricular activities			
Sports			
Clothing			
Education (tutors etc.)			
Subtotal			

Legal		
	Actual Cost	**Projected Cost**	**Difference**
Attorney			
Alimony			
Payments on lien or judgment			
Other			
Subtotal			

Entertainment		
	Actual Cost	**Projected Cost**	**Difference**
Movies			
Dining Out			
Live theater			
Sporting events			
Other			
Other			
Subtotal			

Transportation		
	Actual Cost	**Projected Cost**	**Difference**
Vehicle payment			
Bus/taxi fare			
Insurance			
Fuel			
Maintenance			
Other			
Subtotal			

Taxes		
	Actual Cost	**Projected Cost**	**Difference**
Federal			
State			
Local			
Other			
Subtotal			

Loans			
	Actual Cost	Projected Cost	Difference
Personal			
Education			
Vehicle			
Credit card			
Credit card			
Other			
Subtotal			

Savings or Investments			
	Actual Cost	Projected Cost	Difference
Emergency Savings			
Retirement			
Other			
Other			
Subtotal			

Personal Care			
	Actual Cost	Projected Cost	Difference
Medical			
Hair/nails			
Clothing			
Dry cleaning			
Health club			
Organization dues or fees			
Other			
Subtotal			

Food			
	Actual Cost	**Projected Cost**	**Difference**
Groceries			
Other			
Subtotal			

Pets			
	Actual Cost	**Projected Cost**	**Difference**
Food			
Medical			
Grooming			
Toys			
Other			
Subtotal			

Gifts and Donations			
	Actual Cost	**Projected Cost**	**Difference**
Charity 1			
Charity 2			
Charity 3			
Subtotal			

Total Projected Outlays	
Total Actual Outlays	
Total Difference	

YOUR NEXT STEPS

What is possible for you now that you are no longer preoccupied with money anxiety?

_____

_____

_____

_____

_____

_____

_____

_____

_____

_____

_____

_____

_____

_____

_____

_____

_____

What is the image or object that will help you remember all you have learned here?

_____

_____

_____

_____

_____

List three words that describe how you now feel about your money.

_____

_____

_____

How will you celebrate completing this program?

_____

_____

_____

_____

_____

_____

_____

_____

_____

_____

_____

_____

_____

_____

_____

_____

_____

_____

_____

CONGRATULATIONS!

Notes

Chapter Two

Fidelity Investments. *2021 Couples & Money Survey.* 2021. https://www.fidelity.com/bin-public/060_www_fidelity_com /documents/about-fidelity/Fidelity-Couples-and-Money -Fact-Sheet-2021.pdf.

Lincoln National Corporation. *Lincoln Financial's Consumer Sentiment Tracker.* 2020. https://newsroom.lfg.com/content /1222/files/lincoln_consumer_sentiment_tracking_gender.pdf.

Bank of America. "Bank of America Better Money Habits Research Finds That, Despite Barriers, 80% of Gen Z Are Taking Positive Steps Toward Achieving Their Financial Goals." October 27, 2021. https://newsroom.bankofamerica \.com/content/newsroom/press-releases/2021/10/bank-of -america-better-money-habits-research-finds-that--despite. html.

Bucher-Koenen, Tabea, Rob Alessie, Annamaria Lusardi, and Maarten van Rooij. "Fearless Woman: Financial Literacy and Stock Market Participation." Washington, DC: Global Financial Literacy Excellence Center, March 2021. https://gflec.org /wp-content/uploads/2021/03/Fearless-Woman-Research -March-2021.pdf.

McCrum, Robert. "The 100 best nonfiction books: No 33—The Common Sense Book of Baby and Child Care by Dr Benjamin Spock (1946)." *The Guardian,* September 12, 2016. https://www.theguardian.com/books/2016/sep/12/100-best-nonfiction-books-benjamin-spock-baby-and-child-care.

Anderson, Julie. *Breadwinner Mothers by Race/Ethnicity and State*. Washington, DC: Institute for Women's Policy Research, September 8, 2016. https://iwpr.org/iwpr-issues/esme/breadwinner-mothers-by-race-ethnicity-and-state/.

The Vanguard Group, Inc. *How America Saves 2021.* June 2021. https://institutional.vanguard.com/content/dam/inst/vanguard-has/insights-pdfs/21_CIR_HAS21_HAS_FSreport.pdf.

Snyder, C. R. "Hope Theory: Rainbows in the Mind." *Psychological Inquiry* 13, no. 4 (2002): 249–75. http://www.jstor.org/stable/1448867.

Chapter Three

The Association of International Certified Professional Accountants. *Relationship Intimacy Being Crushed by Financial Tension: AICPA Survey*. 2021. https://www.aicpa.org/news/article/relationship-intimacy-being-crushed-by-financial-tension-aicpa-survey.

Gjelten, E.A. "What Causes Divorce? 8 Common Reasons Marriages End." DivorceNet. Accessed February 8, 2022. https://www.divorcenet.com/resources/common-reasons-marriages-end.html.

National Endowment for Financial Education. "2 in 5 Americans Admit to Financial Infidelity Against Their Partner." November 18, 2021. https://www.nefe.org/news/2021/11/2-in-5-americans-admit-to-financial-infidelity-against-their-partner.aspx.

SunTrust Banks, Inc. "Get Engaged Over The Holiday? It's Time to Set a Date…To Talk About Money." Truist, January 7, 2019.

https://media.truist.com/2019-01-07-Get-Engaged-Over-The-Holiday-Its-Time-to-Set-a-Date-To-Talk-About-Money.

Fidelity Investments. *2021 Couples & Money Survey.* 2021. https://www.fidelity.com/bin-public/060_www_fidelity_com/documents/about-fidelity/Fidelity-Couples-and-Money-Fact-Sheet-2021.pdf.

Hitczenko, Marcin. "The Influence of Gender and Income on the Household Division of Financial Responsibility." Federal Reserve Bank of Boston Research Department Working Papers Series 2016.16-20. October 17, 2016. https://www.bostonfed.org/publications/research-department-working-paper/2016/the-influence-of-gender-and-income-on-the-household-division-of-financial-responsibility.aspx.

UBS. "UBS Own Your Worth report finds that only 20% of couples participate equally in financial decisions." May 6, 2021. https://www.ubs.com/global/en/media/display-page-ndp/en-20210506-own-your-worth.html.

Park, Lora. Associate professor of psychology, State University of New York at Buffalo. Interviewed by author, July 21, 2021.

Chapter Four

Geiger, A.W., Gretchen Livingston, and Kristen Bialik. "6 facts about U.S. moms." Pew Research Center. Last updated May 11, 2017. https://www.pewresearch.org/fact-tank/2019/05/08/facts-about-u-s-mothers/.

U.S Bureau of Labor Statistics. "American Time Use Survey." July 22, 2021. https://www.bls.gov/tus/.

Jones, Janelle. "5 Facts About the State of the Gender Pay Gap." U.S. Department of Labor Blog, March 19, 2021. https://blog.dol.gov/2021/03/19/5-facts-about-the-state-of-the-gender-pay-gap.

Hanson, Melanie. "Student Loan Debt by Gender." Education Data.org, December 16, 2021. https://educationdata.org/student-loan-debt-by-gender.

Chang, Mariko, PhD. "Women and Wealth: Insights for Grantmakers." Asset Funders Network, 2015. https://asset funders.org/wp-content/uploads/Women_Wealth_-Insights _Grantmakers_brief_15.pdf.

Fidelity Investments. *Fidelity Investments Financial Sentiment Survey.* 2021. https://www.fidelity.com/bin-public/060_www _fidelity_com/documents/about-fidelity/FidelityInvestments WomensHistoryMonth.pdf.

Capital Group. "New Capital Group study reveals COVID-19 is shaping women's financial philosophies." April 28, 2021. https://www.capitalgroup.com/about-us/news-room/wisdom -of-experience-womens-financial-philosophies.html.

Wrzesniewski, Amy, Barry Schwartz, Xiangyu Cong, Michael Kane, Audrey Omar, Thomas Kolditz. "Multiple motives don't multiply motivation." *Proceedings of the National Academy of Sciences* 111, no. 30 (July 29, 2014): 10990-10995. https://doi.org/10.1073/pnas.1405298111.

Ben-Shahar, Talal. *Happier.* New York: McGraw Hill, 2007.

Chapter Five

Bank of America. "Bank of America Study Finds 95% of Employers Feel a Sense of Responsibility for Financial Wellness of Employees." September 22, 2021. https://newsroom. bankofamerica.com/content/newsroom/press-releases/2021 /09/bank-of-america-study-finds-95--of-employers-feel-a -sense-of-res.html.

Ohri, Chandni, Catherine New, Helen Robb. "Lack of Savings Has High Cost for Women." BlackRock's Emergency Savings Initiative, March 8, 2021. https://savingsproject.org /lack-of-savings-has-high-cost-for-women/.

Perez, Teresa. "Earnings Peak at Different Ages for Different Demographic Groups." Payscale, June 4, 2019. https://www .payscale.com/research-and-insights/peak-earnings/#overall.

Allred, Colette. "Gray Divorce Rate in the U.S.: Geographic

Variation, 2017." *Family Profiles* no. 20 (2019): 19-20. Bowling Green, OH: National Center for Family & Marriage Research. https://doi.org/10.25035/ncfmr/fp-19-20.

Collinson, Catherine, Patti Rowey, and Heidi Cho. *Life in the COVID-19 Pandemic: Women's Health, Finances, and Retirement Outlook*. Transamerica Center for Retirement Studies, October 2021. https://transamericainstitute.org/docs/default-source/research/women-retirement-security-report.pdf.

Neff, Kristin, PhD. "Exercise 1: How would you treat a friend?" Accessed February 15, 2022. https://self-compassion.org/exercise-1-treat-friend/. Reprinted with permission.

Corless, Roger. *The Vision of Buddhism: The Space under the Tree*. St. Paul: Paragon House, 1998.

Chapter Six

Charles Schwab Corporation. "Schwab Modern Wealth Survey reveals Americans' changing priorities around spending, saving and mental health." 2021. https://www.aboutschwab.com/modern-wealth-survey-2021.

CFP Board. "New Survey Shows Consumers, No Matter Their Income or Assets, Need Support with Spending, Household Budgeting." January 23, 2019. https://www.cfp.net/news/2019/01/new-survey-shows-consumers-no-matter-their-income-or-assets-need-support-with-spending-household.

Starling Bank. "#Make Money Equal." February 2018. https://www.starlingbank.com/docs/reports-research/MakeMoney Equal-Research.pdf.

U.S. Bureau of Labor Statistics. "Consumer Expenditure Surveys." September 9, 2021. https://www.bls.gov/cex/.

Schulz, Matt and Julie Sherrier. "2022 Credit Card Debt Statistics." Lendingtree, February 8, 2022. https://www.lendingtree.com/credit-cards/credit-card-debt-statistics/.

Foster, Sarah. "Survey: More than half of Americans couldn't cover three months of expenses with an emergency fund."

Bankrate, July 21, 2021. https://www.bankrate.com/banking
/savings/emergency-savings-survey-july-2021/

Personal Capital. "The Impact of COVID-19 on Americans'
Nest Egg." January 6, 2021. https://www.personalcapital.com
/blog/retirement-planning/survey-retirement-planning-during
-covid/.

Baker, Andrew. Associate professor of marketing at San Diego
State University. Interviewed by the author, July 21, 2021.

Fidelity Viewpoints. "How much do I need to retire?" August
27, 2021. https://www.fidelity.com/viewpoints/retirement
/how-much-do-i-need-to-retire.

Chapter Seven

Fried, Carla. "What's Your Retirement Number? No, Not
Savings—Life Expectancy." Rate.com, June 28, 2019. https://
www.rate.com/research/news/retirement-expectancy.

The American College of Financial Services. "Focus Female: Study
Shows Big Financial Planning Opportunities for Knowledgeable
Women's Market." January 7, 2021. https://www.theamerican
college.edu/about-the-college/media-center/press-releases
/focus-female-retirement-income-literacy-survey.

Fidelity Investments. *2021 Women and Investing Study*. 2021.
https://www.fidelity.com/bin-public/060_www_fidelity
_com/documents/about-fidelity/FidelityInvestments
Women&InvestingStudy2021.pdf.

Boggio, Cecilia, Elsa Fornero, Henriette M. Prast, and Jose
Sanders. "Seven Ways to Knit Your Portfolio: Is Investor
Communication Neutral?" Netspar Discussion Paper No.
10/2015-030. October 4, 2015. https://papers.ssrn.com/sol3
/papers.cfm?abstract_id=2668579.

Bank of American Corporation. *The financial journey of modern
parenting: Joy, complexity and sacrifice.* 2020. https://mlaem
.fs.ml.com/content/dam/ml/registration/ml_parentstudybro
chure.pdf.

Bureau of Labor Statistics, U.S. Department of Labor. "67 percent of private industry workers had access to retirement plans in 2020." *The Economics Daily,* March 1, 2021. https://www.bls .gov/opub/ted/2021/mobile/67-percent-of-private-industry -workers-had-access-to-retirement-plans-in-2020.htm.

Chapter Eight

El Issa, Erin. "Survey: Less Than Half of Women in U.S. Invest in the Stock Market." Nerdwallet, September 1, 2021. https://www .nerdwallet.com/article/investing/survey-less-than-half-of -women-in-u-s-invest-in-the-stock-market.

Fidelity Investments. *2021 Women and Investing Study.* 2021. https://www.fidelity.com/bin-public/060_www_fidelity _com/documents/about-fidelity/FidelityInvestments Women&InvestingStudy2021.pdf.

Hornsby, Travis, CFA. "Student Loan Debt Statistics in 2022: A Look at The Numbers." Student Loan Planner, December 21, 2021. https://www.studentloanplanner.com/student -loan-debt-statistics-average-student-loan-debt/.

U.S. Department of Education, National Center for Education Statistics. "Tuition costs of colleges and universities." Accessed February 9, 2022. https://nces.ed.gov/fastfacts /displa y.asp?id=76.

U.S. Securities and Exchange Commission. "Bonds." Investor.gov. https://www.investor.gov/introduction-investing/investing -basics/investment-products/bonds-or-fixed-income-products /bonds#Types.

"Treasury Bonds: Tax Considerations." TreasuryDirect. Accessed February 9, 2022. https://www.treasurydirect.gov /indiv/research/indepth/tbonds/res_tbond_tax.htm.

Chapter Nine

Employee Benefit Research Institute. *2021 Retirement Confidence Survey.* 2021. https://www.ebri.org/docs/default-source/rcs /2021-rcs/2021-rcs-summary-report.pdf?sfvrsn=bd83a2f_4.

Social Security Administration. "Retirement Benefits." Accessed February 9, 2022. https://www.ssa.gov/benefits/retirement /planner/delayret.html.

Epilogue

T. Rowe Price. *2021 Parents, Kids & Money Survey.* 2021. https:// www.moneyconfidentkids .com /content /dam/mck/news -and-research/PKM_13thAnnual_2021_deck_Final.pdf.

Harzog, Beverly. "Survey: Majority of Parents Want High Schools to Teach Personal Finance." *U.S. News,* September 8, 2020. https://money.usnews.com/credit-cards/articles /survey-majority-of-parents-want-high-schools-to-teach -personal-finance.

Council for Economic Education. "Survey of the States." February 5, 2020. https://www.council foreconed.org/survey -of-the-states-2020/.

Appendix

Hammer, Alexander R. "Turnover on Stock Market Surges To a New High as Prices Retreat." *The New York Times,* August 19, 1982. https://www.nytimes.com/1982/08/19/business /t urnover-on-stock-market-surges-to-a-new-high-as-prices -retreat.html.

SIFMA Research. *2021 Capital Markets Fact Book.* July 2021. https://www.sifma.org/wp-content/uploads/2021/07/CM -Fact-Book-2021-SIFMA.pdf.

Bogle, John C. "Individual Stockholder, R.I.P." *Wall Street Journal,* October 3, 2005. https://www.wsj.com/articles/SB 112829417598858002.

Parker, Kim and Richard Fry. "More than half of U.S. house-
holds have some investment in the stock market." Pew
Research Center, March 25, 2020. https://www.pewresearch
.org/fact-tank/2020/03/25/more-than-half-of-u-s-house
holds-have-some-investment-in-the-stock-market/.

SPIVA. "Results by Region." Accessed February 9, 2022. https://
www.spglobal.com/spdji/en/res earch-insights/spiva/.

Internal Revenue Service. "Simplified Employee Pension Plan
(SEP)." Last updated January 3, 2022. https://www.irs
.gov/retirement-plans/plan-sponsor/simplified-employee
-pension-plan-sep.

Acknowledgments

You Are Worthy has been a work in progress for many years, and I am grateful to everyone who has helped me bring it to completion.

She Writes Press is a remarkable organization, and I am thrilled to be publishing with them. Brooke Warner is a force of nature—incisive, fair, and supportive all at once. Thank you also to Shannon Green, Samantha Strom, Anne Durette, Cait Levin, and the rest of the team.

After two decades in journalism, I have deep respect for editors who can improve a piece of writing *and* keep writers happy. Marni Seneker and Arielle Eckstudt made all of that happen and more.

Thank you to Susan Adler Funk, Perri Richman, Sally Glick, Claire Toth, Kimberly McPhee, and everyone else who has supported me on my quest to build Own Your Destiny, my coaching and education venture. They have enabled me to work with truly wonderful clients, all of whom have informed this book in some way.

I am also endlessly grateful to the dozens of women who donated their time and shared their private thoughts to help me with my research into women's true feelings and beliefs about money. Your generosity, openness, and willingness to contribute are inspiring. Thank you as well to Sally Coughlin, Juliet Wallace, Sara Ginsberg, Linda Sterling, Pat Berry, and all the friends and colleagues who helped this project come to fruition.

You Are Worthy would never have seen the light of day without the help and support of the incredible writers I am honored to call my friends. Christina Baker Kline introduced me to She Writes Press, and Laura Schenone provided thoughtful and essential feedback early on. I'm also grateful to all the members of my writers' group for their advice, inspiration, and support.

Writing a book is a solitary undertaking, but the support I received from friends and family made it feel anything but. Thank you to Susan Adamsen, Nancy Ylvisaker, Amy Putman, the Dames (you know who you are), John Holland, and Catherine Morsink for providing perspective, encouragement, support, and more than a few laughs. And I need to mention my late parents Norm and Jane, the first writers and editors I ever knew and the people who read my earliest scribbles.

Essential support came from my children in the form of everything from statistical analysis to technical support and dance parties in the kitchen. Henry, Anna, and Eleanor: thank you for motivating me to keep going, and for bolstering my confidence when I needed it most.

And finally, thank you to Steve, for everything you have brought into my life and for your quiet but unwavering belief in this project and in me. When I embarked on this adventure, I failed to understand all I was asking of you, but as ever, you just . . . stepped up. This book would not exist without you.

About the Author

Kelley Holland is the founder and CEO of Own Your Destiny, which provides financial coaching and empowerment programs to help women gain the confidence and knowledge they need to achieve well-being and live life on their terms. She blends her knowledge of finance with communications expertise developed over two decades as an award-winning business and personal finance journalist with *The New York Times, BusinessWeek*, and CNBC. One of her cover stories helped *BusinessWeek* win a National Magazine Award. Kelley has appeared on CNBC, PBS's Frontline, and dozens of radio shows to speak about banking, investing, and personal finance. She graduated from Amherst College and holds a graduate business degree from the Yale School of Management. She is a Chartered Financial Analyst. Kelley lives in northern New Jersey.

Author photo © Michael Stahl

Selected Titles from She Writes Press

⁣‖‖

She Writes Press is an independent publishing
company founded to serve women writers everywhere.
Visit us at www.shewritespress.com.

The Thriver's Edge: Seven Keys to Transform the Way You Live, Love, and Lead by Donna Stoneham. $16.95, 978-1-63152-980-1. A "coach in a book" from master executive coach and leadership expert Dr. Donna Stoneham, The Thriver's Edge outlines a practical road map to breaking free of the barriers keeping you from being everything you're capable of being.

100 Under $100: One Hundred Tools for Empowering Global Women by Betsy Teutsch. $29.95, 978-1-63152-934-4. An inspiring, comprehensive look at the many tools being employed today to empower women in the developing world and help them raise themselves out of poverty.

Think Better. Live Better. 5 Steps to Create the Life You Deserve by Francine Huss. $16.95, 978-1-938314-66-7. With the help of this guide, readers will learn to cultivate more creative thoughts, realign their mindset, and gain a new perspective on life.

This Way Up: Seven Tools for Unleashing Your Creative Self and Transforming Your Life by Patti Clark. $16.95, 978-1-63152-028-0. A story of healing for women who yearn to lead a fuller life, accompanied by a workbook designed to help readers work through personal challenges, discover new inspiration, and harness their creative power.

Supervision Matters: 100 Bite-Sized Ideas to Transform You and Your Team by Rita Sever. $16.95, 978-1-63152-145-4. A collection of practical, accessible, and concise essays offering a comprehensive approach to effective supervision.

Stop Giving it Away: How to Stop Self-Sacrificing and Start Claiming Your Space, Power, and Happiness by Cherilynn Veland. $16.95, 978-1-63152-958-0. An empowering guide designed to help women break free from the trappings of the needs, wants, and whims of other people—and the self-imposed limitations that are keeping them from happiness.